Diary of a
Lollipop
Lady

Hazel Wheeler was born in a Yorkshire village shop, and her fascination with diaries began when she found an old 1936 Police Diary in the attic, which had probably belonged to a Grandad, who was a policeman. She altered the dates to 1941, and began writing in it in pencil from September of that year. The diaries continue to this day.

She left school at 16 with School Certificate credits in Art, History, English Language and English Literature, and passes in French and Biology – but failed the commercial subjects, as expected! She longed to become an artist, and could have worked in an art studio in Leeds, but was too timid to make the daily train journey. She therefore took a number of office jobs before attending Art School for a while, then working in a photographic studio, tinting and 'spotting' photographs.

When her father died suddenly on the eve of his Silver Wedding in 1948, she looked after the family shop until it was sold. Then, with no home and no work, she reluctantly moved in with her mother and new stepfather, continuing to record her daily thoughts and emotions in her diary. The following year she met Granville Wheeler, whose persistence, kindness and sense of humour eventually won her over and they were married in 1952.

Still working in unsatisfying office jobs, she enrolled on a freelance writing course, amazed that people could get paid for writing letters to newspapers and magazines. Her first ever cheque was for a four-sentence letter to the *News Chronicle* headed 'Why I am Happy', under her mother's name, being too self-effacing to use her own. Her father had always been an accomplished letter-writer, often on behalf of customers – perhaps she had inherited his talent. In 1953 she earned four guineas for broadcasting on *Woman's Hour*, introduced by Violet Carson.

Two daughters and many years of money problems, as recounted in this book, followed, until the debts were paid off in the 1980s. Numerous published letters, articles, stories and a regular 'West Riding Letter' in the *Dalesman* magazine later, her first book, *Huddersfield in Old Photographs*, was published in 1989. Two more old photograph books, *Huddersfield at War* and *Pennine People*, followed. *Half a Pound of Tuppenny Rise* recounted life in the family shop, *The Milliner's Apprentice* told of her mother's Edwardian girlhood in Boroughbridge, and *Sing a Song of Sixpence* described childhood in 1920s, '30s and '40s Yorkshire. *Living on Tick*, the sequel to *Tuppenny Rice*, followed *Huddersfield, The Old Days*. In 2004, *First of the Summer Wine* described Bamforths sentimental song and hymn cards and the local people who posed for them, and featured Holmfirth scenes, photos of 'Compo', 'Nora Batty' and 'Foggy', and a Foreword by Roy Clarke.

Granville died from lung cancer in 1999, probably as a result of working in pubs for years to help pay off the moneylenders. Hazel moved south to be nearer her two daughters, but longs to return to her native Yorkshire.

Diary of a
Lollipop
Lady

Memories of a
crossing patrol in the 1960s

Hazel
Wheeler

• A SILVER LINK BOOK •
from
The NOSTALGIA Collection

To Lollipop Ladies – and Gentlemen – past and present
who boarded 'The Good Ship Lollipop'.
May they have no harder landing than 'on a chocolate bar'!

© Hazel Wheeler 2005

*All rights reserved. No part of this publication may be reproduced, stored in a
retrieval system or transmitted, in any form or by any means, electronic, mechanical,
photocopying, recording or otherwise, without prior permission in writing from
Silver Link Publishing Ltd.*

First published in 2005

British Library Cataloguing in Publication Data

A catalogue record for this book is available from the British Library.

ISBN 1 85794 266 3

Silver Link Publishing Ltd
The Trundle
Ringstead Road
Great Addington
Kettering
Northants NN14 4BW

Tel/Fax: 01536 330588
email: sales@nostalgiacollection.com
Website: www.nostalgiacollection.com

Printed and bound in Great Britain

Contents

Introduction   7

1   'When I first put this uniform on...'   9
2   'Aren't you nervous?'   14
3   Mad March winds   20
4   Hope springs eternal   28
5   Sweet charity   34
6   Raining, cats and dogs   39
7   Holiday blues   45
8   Excursions and alarms   51
9   Magic moments   57
10 '...noted for fresh air and fun'   62
11 The electrician cometh   68
12 Chapter of accidents   74
13 Counting blessings   81
14 Waifs and strays   86
15 'Some folk get all the bad luck...'   90
16 Windy, itchy weather   97
17 Deadlock on the crossing   104
18 Prize-winners   110
19 'Roll on Christmas!'   116
20 Bullies   122
21 'There's allus summat afore Christmas for
        somebody...'   128
22 Home cooking   134
23 Anticipation   139
24 Christmas spirit   145
25 End of term   151
26 ''Twas the night before Christmas...'   157
27 Ring in the new   163
28 The cavalcade is over   171

'Whether the weather be fine,
Or whether the weather be not,
Whether the weather be cold
Or whether the weather be hot –
We'll weather the weather,
Whatever the weather –
Whether we like it nor not!'

Introduction

I dread to think what our black-gowned, pince-nez-wearing headmistress at the girls' grammar school I attended during the war years – Greenhead High School, Huddersfield – would have thought about one of 'her girls' turning out to be a Lollipop Lady. Most of them went on after School Certificate, then Higher School Certificate, to become BAs or achieve other high-falutin status, not a BF – bloody fool.

Since being married there had been a scarcity of cash and an abundance of bills, leaving no loophole for my yearning for excitement, adventure and change. Indeed, having had a series of house moves, all at a financial loss because I couldn't stand another minute of neighbours, resulted in financial disaster. Unknown to me, my at-his-wits-end husband became hopelessly entangled with moneylenders, borrowing from new ones to pay off ever more demanding earlier ones. Finding a full-time job myself was out of the question. Our two young daughters steadfastly refused to stay for school dinners. The only time I had insisted, they had hid behind duffle coats in the cloakroom at dinnertime. So I was paying for something they hadn't had, then having to provide something more substantial at teatime, to make up for the long fast from breakfast.

'Make 'em stay,' advised friends, scuttling back to work at breakneck speed once their offspring were at school. 'They'll get used to it.'

But I hated making children do what I had never done, and also would have hated. So bills kept coming – and so did men at the door, asking to see my husband 'on an urgent matter', and taking away the TV set. I began to wonder if one day they'd take me too.

My nerves were frayed, and so were the children's. Even the cat dashed out of reach beneath the table when the doorbell rang; though only a stray, she was obviously putting a high price on herself, suspecting that as everything else seemed to be being taken away, her time would come too.

Some mums worked as school dinner ladies to earn a bit of extra, but I hated the idea. Besides, I wouldn't have been at home during the crucial midday mealtime. And it sounded too much like what I had to do at home, extremely dull and dreary – no excitement.

So, when the ancient Lollipop Man who shepherded schoolchildren across the busy and dangerous main road packed the job in, I passed a sleepless night wondering if I dare take his place. It would provide some much-needed money, I'd be able to give Elizabeth and Caroline a midday snack, then see them safely across the road again – and be paid for it. I already took them every crossing time as it was – each morning, collected them at midday, back again, then at teatime. A bit like a mother hen, I often took other mothers' children as well, when they couldn't be bothered. I can't imagine what it must be like having a placid disposition!

Next morning, before I'd time to change my mind, I caught a bus to town and offered my services at the Education Offices as the new Wakefield Road crossing Lollipop Lady. All eight stones, five feet four of me. My predecessor had been of the barrage balloon build, but I was welcomed with open arms. Even then few were willing to risk their lives for £3 14s 6d a week.

Could I begin next day, they asked. My mouth went dry and parched with apprehension, but I smiled brightly and croaked, 'Yes, certainly.'

1

'When I first put this uniform on...'

No wonder people weren't rushing to be crossing wardens, I thought ruefully next morning, a foggy first of February. I stood at the end of our lane, enveloped in a floor-sweeping, white plastic coat with huge wide sleeves, allowing snow and rain to trickle down as I held up the Lollipop pole. The collar, turned up, cut into my face as I turned left and right watching the traffic.

It was an unearthly hour for me to be at large, eight thirty, and 'large' was the operative word as the intense cold stiffened out the plastic mac, giving me an unnaturally rotund shape. I hoped I'd be able to hide my face in the collar, as a tortoise does when it pulls back inside its shell, if anyone I knew walked by.

The damp grey mist swirled round my jaunty navy beret, adding to the effect of a French Resistance fighter of the 'forties. I'd been issued with navy woollen gloves – Large Men's – and stub-toed heavy wellingtons completed the inelegant picture. They'd forgotten to provide a belt, so I looked quite nine months pregnant. But there was no time to do anything about it. My new charges would be appearing at any time, and would expect someone in authority to escort them across the road. I didn't want to be accused of negligence on the first morning.

I stood holding the 'STOP, CHILDREN' pole as inconspicuously as possible behind my back, leaning against the damp, cold, stone wall, waiting until my policeman tutor arrived. Standing there all alone, that ridiculous song from the Gilbert and Sullivan operetta rang through my mind:

> 'When I first put this uniform on, I said as I looked in the
>   glass,
> It's one to a million, that any civilian
> My figure or form could surpass...'

Then my policeman tutor swaggered round the corner. A handsome, broad-shouldered, swashbuckling figure, he walked with an attractive joie de vivre attitude.

'Morning!' he beamed, touching his helmet in greeting, and grinning and winking at me as the first vehicle slowly went by – a black shiny hearse bearing two top-hatted gentlemen and a pale oak coffin.

'All life is vanity,' observed my new friend. 'In the twinkling of an eye we are in death. But why worry? Do you want a Polo?' He flicked open a packet and popped a mint into his mouth.

'Ee, Hazel, what are *you* doing here?' queried fussy little Mrs Costa, who was admirably suited to living by the main road – able to see, and hear, everything that was going on, who bought bread at Mr Wood's instead of Hatfields, who visited the Stag pub, and how often, who disappeared inside the shrieking, whining ambulances. 'Oh, ta,' she continued, accepting the policeman's offer of a Polo, and giving me no time to explain about my longing for excitement, adventure and change – plus a little extra money.

'Well, ah looked out of our lavatory window this morning and said to our Harry, "D'you know lad, I'm sure it's a woman on t'crossing now..."'

By now news was spreading like wildfire that 'Mrs Wheeler from up t'lane had turned into a Lollipop Lady,' and everybody was coming for a look. Then my very first customer, a small girl of about five or six, thrust her cold little hand into mine.

'Ooh, Mrs Lollipop, I'm *freezing!*'

My policeman stood back and watched as I ventured forth for the first time. Pole held high, feeling like Boadicea may have felt, marching into battle.

But the year was 1966. It didn't help my wildly beating heart when a bread van slowly paused and the driver gave a long, low wolf whistle – and chucked a big stale loaf at my feet.

'Share it wi' t'other birds, luv,' he shouted.

I put it on the wall to share with any birds in quiet moments.

Next, a crowd of small boys loomed out of the mist, saucer-eyed with amazement that the usual Barrage Balloon man had disappeared, and a different apparition had taken his place.

'Hey, it's a lady!' the first comer yelled to his pals. At least he hadn't said woman. I'd have shrunk further into my collar then, and felt like a lavatory attendant on her first morning – far from flushed with success.

I realised I was not doing the older boys any favour by attempting to hold *their* hands. Smaller ones were friendlier, giving me a warm glow of acting as a surrogate mother.

Wendy, who lived up our lane, shuffled up to me, huge, hand-knitted red scarf up to her big, blue eyes against the bitterly cold morning.

'There's me as well,' six-year-old Martin, her brother, reminded me as I smiled a greeting and held out my hand.

Before half past nine I had spoken to more people than I normally did during the course of a week. And more compliments had come my way than I'd had since courting.

'Ee, ah do admire your pluck!' gasped one elderly lady, thumping me appreciatively on the back. 'Ah wouldn't do this job for a thousand pounds a week.'

Another ambled up, aided with a walking stick, grey-faced and grey-haired, like the weather, the sort who seem to have lost the art of smiling.

'Ah didn't fancy asking yon other, you understand,' explaining her predicament. 'Him being a man and all that. Fact is, I'm terrified of crossing roads, especially busy uns like this. Me sister is allus telling me to go into town and spend a whole morning on the crossings, backwards and forwards, till I feel I can manage with me eyes shut. What d'you think?'

The policeman grabbed her shapeless, tweed-coated waist.

'Come here, luv. I suggest we begin by going across this one doing a set of the Lancers. Leaping high in the air when a number 73 comes in sight. Then making a dash for the other side.'

'Gerroff, yer silly thing,' Grey Face objected, twisting from his grasp. 'It's her ah was talking to, not you.'

A great glow of achievement overwhelmed me as the fog closed in again shortly before I took the icy cold Lollipop behind the back of the little grocery shop at the end of my first day.

Four thirty. I'd survived! I was still intact, and confident and enthusiastic about what the morrow may bring. What a lot I had to tell Granville, Elizabeth, Caroline, and, of course, Prince, our female tabby cat (all our pets having proudly borne the name Prince whether male or female).

The next morning brought rain, and, to my sorrow, a different policeman. I'd half fallen in love with the bouncy, full-of-fun first one, and even dreamed about him in bed. But we weren't on a school crossing in a February mist.

The new one was concerned only about the job being done to the letter, and was haughty and huffy, especially when he tried to make me hold the pole differently. Lollipop and I had already formed a kind of rapport, a bit like Laurel and Hardy. I felt right with the pole as we were. I retained my hold on it.

'I'll be quite all right by myself,' I retorted, as icily as the weather, and mentally adding, 'and you can scram as far as I'm concerned.'

'All right then, if you can manage,' he sniffed, and off he went. I always did prefer being my own boss, and now here I was, boss of the whole main road crossing! No wonder Hitler strove for World Power – already I was beginning to appreciate what I suppose motivated him. Talk about wielding the Big Stick! Me – until that week usually making the beds in my old blue dressing-gown at eight thirty in the morning, or feeding the cat – now in charge of a main road crossing!

And when passers-by stopped passing to talk with me, didn't I hear some tales...

"Ullo, love – ooh, ah don't feel well at all today,' moaned Kathy, out early to get the shopping done. 'Ah've got this 'ere bubble on me bowel, yer see.'

The bemused expression I assumed encouraged further confidences.

'Me doctor likes to give me the once-over every so often,' she continued, an agonised grimace on her rouged face. 'And seeing I'm under him he should know, shouldn't he? You don't mind me talking to you like this, do you?'

'Oh, not at all,' I replied. 'It's very interesting. I do hope the bubble bursts before long...'

'Ee, ah don't know about that, Hazel – I don't know whether it's supposed to burst or just go on lying there, dormant kind of thing.'

I had to stand there an hour every morning, half past eight until half past nine. So when anyone wanted to talk, I was more than pleased to listen. It made the periods when there were no children to take across much more interesting. I could hardly be seen standing reading a book, or knitting.

The first policeman had given me a copy of the *Highway Code* to study. But I was completely mystified by the multiplicity of hand signs given. All kinds of signs. They could have meant practically anything – and probably did, by the accompanying leer on some of the faces zooming past.

But I smiled at each one, now more or less the sex symbol of the crossing, and hoped I wasn't condoning outright rudeness while trying to look intelligent at the same time.

The General Public, motorists, lorry drivers, coal wagon drivers, everybody, expected the Lollipop Lady to be something of a Geographical Know-all. 'Hoi, lass, am I all right for Holmfirth?' 'How far to Huddersfield?' 'Which way to Wakefield?' or 'What times does paper shop shut at Waterloo?' And a facetious query from one coal wagon driver as he drew up at my crossing to allow me to take a crowd of juniors across:

'Lollipop!' he bawled, white teeth in a black face, 'where do yer garage yer Lollipop?' But there was no time to think up witty retorts before the Wit of the Moment was speeding on his way.

I wondered why it was that outdoor workers appeared so much more contented with their lot than frenzied office workers. While the latter were dashing for the eight-forty into town, John, the elderly, ruddy-faced gardener, whose huge wart at the side of his nose only enhanced his genial appearance, sauntered in a leisurely fashion along the pavement, work-worn hands thrust deep into the pockets of comfortable corduroy trousers. The fact that his tummy bulged heavily over the leather belt that held them up did nothing to detract from his general air of likeability.

'Well, 'ow at ah lass?' was his daily greeting. The warmth of his brick-coloured face and smile helped thaw out the bitterest winter day. Then he crossed over to the little grocery store run by pale, anaemic-looking, thirty-ish Nellie for cigarettes and a box of matches, jostling in the doorway with her as he tried to snatch a good-natured kiss to begin the day.

His job, gardener and general odd-job man at the Corporation Old Folks' bungalows, was not one where he'd make riches. Yet he enjoyed a quality of life far surpassed by that of merely making money. John was always ready to lend a helping hand to anyone, and was universally respected and loved. *Real* riches.

2

'Aren't you nervous?'

*A*fter the dismal mists and fogs at the beginning of the week came high winds and lashing rain – gale-force winds that made it nigh impossible to hold Lollipop upright. It lurched uncontrollably all over the road like a drunken man. On a few occasions, with gusts of wind and rain battering relentlessly at my face and traffic roaring by, sending torrents of rainwater way up my wellingtons, I glanced up at the Belisha beacon posts halfway across the road with the vague idea that if life became too hectic at ground level I could, perhaps, scrim up there for a moment's respite. My predecessor-but-one had been blown to the ground during a ferocious gale, but he was older and frailer than either me or the Barrage Balloon warden.

The first week over, I knew most people's comings and goings, which cat and dog belonged to which family, who went out to work and where, and which child belonged to which mother. How worried I felt for some, whose mothers went out to work and sometimes missed the usual bus home, leaving children hanging about in the cold, waiting for them if they had forgotten, or didn't have, a key. And bedraggled, sad-eyed cats and dogs, flopping eagerly after home-coming owners following long, miserable hours left to their own devices outdoors. 'In the bleak mid winter.'

Being outside in slush, snow and driving winds, thunder and lightning, if only for three hours a day, five days a week, made me sorrier than ever for strays. At least I could measure the sometimes tortuous times of numb fingertips and toes by glancing at my watch, knowing that five minutes had passed, then half an hour, and so on, until time to thankfully dash up home, face glowing, delight surging all over me as I turned the key in the lock. No such respite for strays, or those with insensitive, uncaring owners.

I could poke the fire into a welcoming blaze, throwing a log on for the cat to appreciate as well as myself, put the kettle on for a steaming cup of coffee – or two, or three, or even four – and maybe a couple of fat jam doughnuts to help the thawing-out process. Prince could enjoy a saucer of warm milk as I read a magazine and looked at pictures of fur-coat-clad models stepping out of ritzy cars, and pondered the difference between those lives and my own.

But oh, how I pitied those strays, and animals left out all day! Our cat luxuriated in winter. She tentatively shot out (with the gentle help of a little shove) into the bleak back garden to relieve herself, then appeared, wild-eyed, at the back window, hoping against hope that I hadn't gone to the crossing again before letting her in to rejoin her cosy, hair-covered armchair at the side of the fire.

Those callous types who shrug off the sight of pathetic animals shivering, hungry and unwanted in our inhospitable British winters ought to be forced to try an outdoor job for a while, in the very depths of winter. Maybe that would warm their hearts to those dejected creatures. There's nothing quite like being in another person's shoes – or paws – for finding out what it really feels like to be helpless in those circumstances.

You also meet the 'haves' as well as the 'have nots' of this life while performing a public duty – those who are so well fed that it sometimes upsets their ego and becomes a problem. Katie, a svelte, thirty-ish girl who spent much of her waking hours reading diet sheets, told me that she'd hit on a method whereby she didn't think she'd have to abandon her mid-morning cream cakes.

'I've decided to cut out lunch completely, Hazel,' she confided. Her ambition was to appear as slim and provocative to her 'super boss' as her younger, teenage workmates. I became her unofficial slimming advisor. Turning her back on the bus queue, to our left, she unbuttoned her coat daily and gazed at me with anxious, hopeful, big, brown eyes.

'Am I losing it, Hazel? Do you think so – do you *really* think so?'

If one of my 'customers' sauntered up for me to take them across the road she would dodge back and stand waiting against the wall.

'It's all right – I can catch the next bus. I think it's a good idea to let someone other than a friend decide. They don't tell the truth all the time, do they?'

I must admit that, friend or foe, I did become rather at a loss for new adjectives to admire her diminishing form. And what would regulars of the one fifteen bus think this woman was showing me every day? Perhaps they might think she was a female flasher...

Valentine's Day came and I was still keeping the snow and icicles company. I was told by one policeman that it was something of a rarity for a woman to stick the job for more than a week. During a lull between children wanting to cross, the young policeman, riding a bicycle, drew up to the kerb gazing at me with quizzical eyes.

'Aren't you nervous?' he asked. 'All the blokes we've had threatened to pack it in after the first week. A few people have been killed at this crossing, you know. We've only had one woman doing the job before you. She was terrified out of her wits and left after two days.'

He went on to tell me about the OAP Lollipop Man who had been killed three or four years ago. My blood felt more chilled than before as he cycled merrily on his way. Perhaps he thought it his duty to tell me. But I'd rather not have known. It wouldn't be worth the £3 14s 6d a week (with half-pay during school holidays) if my daughters were left motherless. I began to wonder how my obituary might be phrased: 'Lollipop Lady Mangled to Pulp by Coal Lorry' – 'Lollipop Lady Gives Life for her Charges' – 'Lollipop Lady for Posthumous VC'…

Leaning against the cold, stone wall, lost in idle reverie, my eyes filled with tears of self-pity as I imagined the scene – Granville prostrate with grief, Elizabeth and Caroline hysterical, Prince wildly chasing her own tail trying vainly to find me, and Roddy, her pal, joining in. And me, lying pale, heroic and beautiful in death… Then I'd have to hurriedly pull myself together from my daydream as I felt a pull at my coat, and off we plodded to the other side of the road.

It had been a cold winter, more so than usual, and the coal in our cellar hadn't lasted as long as we'd hoped. It might have done had I followed my husband's advice, and allowed the fire to die down when I was out, instead of piling more coal on for the cat, and Roddy, the one from the bungalow opposite who came in to snuggle down in the big doll's pram at the opposite side of the fireplace. Roddy's family all went out to work, but it was all right for him as there was always a welcome in the doll's pram, and food to share with Prince.

Our coalman wasn't due to deliver for another week. It was mid-February and there was only a scraping of coal left in the cellar. I set about discovering some of the perks of a Lollipop Lady's job – by now, you will have gathered, dignity was a thing of the past, as were all my inhibitions about being seen in the Lollipop garb, and what people might think – 'Is that the best she can do? Must be hard up.' Well, I was. But I was doing something about it, and helping others into the bargain. It suited my purposes for the time being, and that was all that mattered.

Anyway, I was beginning to think of myself as something akin to one of 'the Few' from the Battle of Britain. The navy beret was quite jaunty, my skin had lost its usual indoor pallor, and men were obviously interested in Lollipop at the end of the lane – if one uses one's imagination it's easy to visualise a wonderful role for oneself in the most menial of jobs.

Earlier daydreams, in my teens, before money was a consideration, were of being knocked down by a car – not injured enough to mar my looks –

and Errol Flynn, or maybe Charles Boyer, springing out from – well, it didn't matter where from – scooping me up in their arms and kissing me 'to make it better'. I never *could* decide who I'd prefer...

But now, reality. Here was a challenge I couldn't have met stuck in an office. I was in the heroic position of being able to provide winter fuel with my own Large Men's navy-clad hands. Past the corner where I positioned myself and my pole (yes, I'd become quite emotionally attached to Pole, as one does with a car, which of course for us was way beyond our wildest dreams, although in imagination you can take a rainbow-ride on a pole) scores of coal lorries lumbered by, spilling their jet-black cargo at my feet (and, at less pleasant moments, dust in my eyes).

Desperate situations call for desperate measures, so I took a couple of old enamel buckets and a shovel down to the crossing each session, opting for slight embarrassment rather than shivering in the evening at home. With an old fireside brush and the buckets against the wall by Pole, I was all ready for action. There were the usual cocky, predictable comments from certain passers-by, those with central heating, which we didn't have. 'What's up lass – ah yer gonna be sick?' 'Atta freetened o' being taken short, Lollipop?'

But the strategy worked. In between taking the children across I busily brushed coal into the waiting buckets, never imagining that I'd descend to being a road sweeper as well as a Lollipop Lady. I glowed with pride as I carried the full buckets up the lane after each session.

My luck was in on the last duty of the day – a chivalrous coalman drew up and smiled so kindly.

'Na then, Lollipop, how about if I drop thi a couple of bags to put you on? Give me your address and I'll leave them by your coal grate.'

What price Errol Flynn, Charles Boyer, or even Nelson Eddy singing 'Sweetheart' to Jeannette MacDonald? That grimy-faced coalman was my hero of the hour, and I kissed him on his cheek, thanking him profusely. A friend for life.

I felt inordinately proud when my husband shivered up the lane from work, looking like a long, thin snowman with worried lines across his forehead.

'What are we going to do about a fire?' he asked.

'Look in the cellar and find out,' I smirked as I doled out dollops of thick, aromatic Irish stew. The look of adoration that Granville flashed at me was, I'm sure, more meant than on our wedding day!

Despite the amount of traffic that passed 'my' crossing, accidents were a rarity. But near ones occurred frequently. Slanging matches between motorists often enlivened a day, and frequently the displays of temper by both drivers and pedestrians were funny in the extreme.

I'll never forget the time two private cars bumped into each other. No one was physically hurt, but feelings most definitely were. Two highly flushed gentlemen sprang out of each car, locking arms in combat for all the world like an old Charlie Chaplin film. Fists were clenched, so were teeth. Like mad dogs, they leaped at each other's throats, shouting four-letter abuse until a policeman zoomed alongside on a motor bike. It always baffled me the way the Law somehow managed to loom up as from nowhere in a crisis.

What a metamorphosis takes place at the sight of a uniform, and a few calming words from an uninvolved party. Blood pressures visibly dropped, and within seconds the two erstwhile arch-enemies were grinning broadly and patting each other on the back. Anger does more to cause actual physical damage than all the road accidents put together.

I also encountered a number of bullies among the children. Drama was commonplace on the crossing. One tiny tot came hurtling back to me a few minutes after being safely shepherded across.

'Miss!' – some of them called me 'Miss', not yet knowing my name – 'Miss, that ginger boy, he hit me. And then – and then –' eyes opening wider and overflowing with huge tears, 'and then he tried to strangle me!'

I could always tell who the bullies were by the way they treated their toys. One portly small boy, whose stocky figure and warlike eye caused other five-year-olds to scatter on sight, sometimes brought his battered old Teddy to school. Occasionally poor Teddy arrived having been kicked there all the way. I'm sure everything has feelings, even old stuffed Teddies. So, anxious to try and make friends in my now omnipotent role as Mistress of the Crossing and all that went on it, I made enquiries about poor old Ted.

'I wonder why Teddy groans like?' I asked the young bully one morning. He stuck a bright pink tongue out at me.

''Cos ah'm allus picking 'im up by t'ear,' came the off-putting reply. I could cheerfully have picked that cheeky little devil up by *his* ear and flung him under the oncoming bus. Nevertheless, Andrew, as I found he was called, became a staunch friend, and proved that friendship as the winter days slipped into spring by offering me freshly caught frogs, alive, alive-o. There was a swampy area in the field opposite the lane, a favourite hunting ground with little boys on their way to and from school. Sometimes, in wet weather, walking back up the lane I'd have to smartly side-step a bulbous frog that had hopped its way from the field.

The frog offering from Andrew became a tricky situation. I didn't want to offend him, and rightly guessed that for him to even consider parting with one of his slimy fat prizes in slithery plastic bags, crude holes punched in the sides for ventilation, was an honour indeed. I evaded the situation where I envisaged jam jars full of frogs and tadpoles piling up on the crossing for me by bestowing unlimited admiration on the captives – from a distance – and telling Andrew that, what a shame, but our cat, Prince, adored frogs with fresh cream for her tea. And we must never hurt living things, must we?

Indeed, I pursued quite a crusade in the cause of kindness to animals while I had such an ideal opportunity to instil good behaviour in everyone and everything down on the crossing. I hoped that other, future Lollipop people would do the same, not merely standing with the children silently until it was time to cross. Yet I found it difficult to bear kind feelings to the lad who slipped a vivacious, zippy frog down the top of my wide wellington boot as I set off into the centre of the road, with a long line of traffic either side. The lad was still roaring with laughter when he reappeared up the snicket from school at teatime.

Or ever to trust young Debbie again, with her sweet, innocent-looking face framed by black hair and a fringe. On one of the warmer March days when I left the Large Men's gloves at home, Debbie smiled up at me and slipped her hand into mine. It felt strange. Then Debbie, giggling, removed her hand, having pressed a long red wriggly earthworm into the palm of my hand. Ugh! Never, in all my life, had I dared to touch a worm when helping in our garden. Indeed, when digging up potatoes one morning I'd asked the dustbin man if he'd dig the rest of them up for me as I hated even the sight of those squirming objects. Now here was one stuck to my hand – shaking it didn't seem to budge it, and I couldn't face lifting it off with the other hand. And a bus was coming, and another group of children.

Never had I been more delighted to spy Andrew among them. 'Andrew, please can you get this horrible thing off my hand?' I pleaded.

No sooner said than done.

'You're not nervous about traffic, Lollipop, yet you daren't even touch a bit of a worm,' he grinned as he chucked it into a garden along the main road.

No amount of washing and scrubbing my hands with pan cleaners when I got home again could dispel that awful wormy feeling.

3

Mad March winds

*I*f I forgot to wear my wristwatch I had to keep asking 'What time is it, please?' to passers-by, reminding me of that childhood game 'What time is it, Mr Wolf?' We crept up behind Mr Wolf until he or she yelled, 'Dinnertime!', when all of us flew back to avoid capture.

Soon, however, I could almost tell the time by when people went to work, or took their dogs to do the necessary before the poor creatures were locked indoors again when they went to work. Until other events took my mind off those dogs, I imagined their dismay when their owner locked the door behind them. If they hadn't a window to look out of, how on earth would they pass the long lonely hours?

Regular as clockwork, panting along the pavement where I stood with my pole, diminutive In-a-Big-Hurry man in his long raincoat rushed by with two down-to-earth black dachshunds. He reminded me of a charioteer, the way he held the dog leads and was pulled along by them. First I'd sense a breathless feeling in the air, then appeared the three brisk comrades out for their morning airing, pink tongues dropping moisture on to the pavement, their owner still in carpet slippers unless it was raining or snowing. His narrow face sported a little fair clipped moustache that matched his short back and sides. The balding patch at the back passed me at nine o'clock exactly, before the trio disappeared further down the road into the local park.

Though rules were always to carry the 'STOP – CHILDREN' pole when going across the road, when mad March winds unleashed their fury I took the law into my own hands. When I found that the pole, waving all over the place in a gale-force wind, was tending rather to knock children out and give them a crack on the head than protect them when I was unable to control it, I laid it down alongside the wall.

Sometimes the wind howled round that northern corner with such ferocity and brute strength that keeping *myself* upright and my beret on my head was all I could manage. Occasionally flashes of lightning and thunder added to the growing panic among the children, and me. Quite oblivious to setting an example to the young at those moments, I often snarled, 'Blasted moneylenders! What a bloody job – I'll pack the whole thing in and to Hell with everything.'

Yet we staggered across to the other side, cars swerving to sudden halts in their pell-mell effort to get away from the storm, sending up high tides of rainwater and completely soaking me through, despite my Antarctic outfit. My hair really was like dripping wet rats' tails on such duties, and I could lick the rainwater as it cascaded down my face.

It was ironic how the elements determinedly reserved their worst until half past eight in the morning, five to twelve noon, or three-thirty in the afternoon. On such crossings how I envied Prince, snoozing happily in the chair by the fire, pink tongue stuck out in complete oblivion.

The weather had an adverse effect on our front door too. I'd had another key made for nine-year-old Caroline so she could let herself in while I was on duty at the end of our lane (by that time Elizabeth was at another school, too far away to return home at midday). I felt terribly guilty sometimes when I dashed back up the lane at half past twelve to find her still standing under the porch while rain splashed miserably round her. She was that bit too small to put enough force into turning the key, even if standing on tip-toes. A few times she managed it, at others plucking up the courage to ask the young man a couple of doors above our house if he'd mind turning the key. How infuriating to see her out in the cold while Prince the cat was warm as an Indian summer inside!

However, it wasn't all plain sailing when she managed to join Prince indoors. The cat loved us all, I'm sure, but why did she have to sneak up on Caroline from beneath her chair and bite her ankles when she had her to herself? Or when the coalman or other person knocked loudly on the door just when Caroline was inside alone, I'd find her huddled in a frightened heap beneath the table. Maybe she thought it one of those dreaded moneylender men. Her Dad didn't know how to cope with them, and she certainly couldn't. I had warned both girls never to open the door to anyone.

Yet fear could also come via the telephone. A white-faced Caroline opened the door for me one dinnertime as I brought back fish and chips from the shop opposite the crossing.

'Mummy, the telephone rang and a man said (sob), "You will die tonight" – then he put the phone down. I daren't go to sleep in case I do –'

I reassured her that some people have nothing more interesting to do than make stupid phone calls, and that fish and chips, eaten while hot, are far more important than such silly people.

Such happenings are the disadvantages of being a working mother, which many take in their stride in their quest for money. Yet every time coalman, car or anonymous phone call struck, I vowed to give up being a Lollipop Lady. Let the bailiffs come, let anything happen rather than have my children terrified out of their wits.

Then the flicker of early spring sunshine, or the sight of the first snowdrop in a garden as I dashed back down the lane – then yellow and mauve crocuses nodding brightly in the breeze – made me realise how much I enjoyed the job. Out in the fresh air regularly, and paid for it, I was my own boss, and, best of all, not confined in a dreary office, maybe having to work day in, day out, with colleagues I did not like. On the crossing there was variety, lots of laughter, and I didn't even have bus fares to pay. I never knew from one moment to the next what might happen. So yes, it wasn't a posh job, or one I'd boast about to a social climbing type of person. But I don't like that type of person anyway. And it was giving me a kind of excitement, and certainly change.

Besides, the £3 14s 6d I earned each week was wonderful after not earning a regular wage for years! Freelance writing brought an occasional guinea cheque for a letter to a magazine, but one day I hoped that my 'Diary of a Lollipop Lady' would make all the soakings, and difficulties, worthwhile.

Elizabeth and Caroline were growing up fast, and would soon probably be wanting pretty clothes and spending money. They never asked for anything, knowing the financial situation all too well. That was the main reason I didn't want them to not enjoy what others had – because they never asked.

One evening Granville and I went to the Open Day at Elizabeth's school. The English teacher remarked how good Elizabeth's latest essay had been, about two letters in a post-box falling in love, then having to be parted. Well, if her thoughts at twelve years old were dwelling on thoughts of love and marriage, we'd need some money for a wedding before long! A parent is pulled so many ways when there are children – wanting to stay at home to look after them, wanting to give them material advantages. But how to decide?

I didn't dare dwell on the predicament we were in because of the exorbitant interest rates those moneylenders were extracting from my husband. Otherwise I may have picked up the sharpest kitchen knife we had, hidden it beneath my white plastic Lollipop coat, gone into town, to their offices, and plunged the knife into the cold, callous things they cared to call hearts. In calmer moments, of course, I realised that a crime of passion never solves a problem. Who would look after the children if I was in jail?

It was knives – well, shears – that had plunged us into this financial dilemma to start with. There was a flimsy, useless fence between our first house and that of a neighbour, and the next-door toddler had access to their garden shed, and daily poked shears and other lethal garden objects at Elizabeth when she was too young to understand the danger and keep clear. I threatened my husband if he didn't put up a sturdy, impervious fence to stop my worries about Elizabeth being blinded, he could put the house up for sale. Rather than let the neighbours think he was being awkward, erecting a fence between us that couldn't be penetrated with shears and all the rest of it, Granville chose to move. We sold, at a loss. The new house was too expensive, so then we had to sell that house – how tangled the paths that lead us into totally unexpected ways of life!

We had married in 1952, and 1953 was when the first school crossing patrols began. I'd never have believed it if I'd been told then that one day I'd be wearing the distinctive white coat and carrying a crossing pole! Yet I was enjoying most of the time better than any other job I'd had!

However, it was now 1966, and there was only one way to go, plodding on as I was, and Granville working in pubs as a waiter in the evenings after his daytime job to pay money to the parasites who prey on the misfortune of others.

Anyway, after being within the cloisters of home for so long, with the milkman the only male I spoke to apart from my husband, I was beginning to feel again the flirty flutterings of youth on the crossing. Some of those handsome policemen, luscious lorry drivers and suave motorists were turning my head in more ways than one.

Well, it's such an upheaval to be winked at so early in a morning – but so invigorating, especially after a routine weekend of catching up with the chores. I was enjoying putting lipstick on again first thing in the morning, wondering who I'd see. Some of the motorists were really sexy looking, and made me feel I wouldn't mind being made love to right there on the crossing.

One morning I must have been more flustered than usual because after the first stint of the day, after I'd 'garaged' the pole down the snicket behind Nellie's shop, I tripped up over the pavement edge, falling flat on my face in front of a full line-up of traffic. I couldn't decide whether I'd look sillier smiling as if nothing had happened, or doing what came naturally and uttering a load of oaths. However, I brushed the mud off my coat and tried to disappear up the lane with as much dignity as possible. Well, I mean, thirty-nine and acting like a lovesick teenager just because a tantalising face behind a steering wheel had smiled at me. But then, we didn't have a car, and motorists were, in my mind, a kind of aristocracy. It must be wonderful to have a car, and the freedom to go anywhere one fancied, rather than being a fixture by a bus stop, standing with a 'STOP – CHILDREN' pole in hand as I did.

One mild, clear day of cloudless blue skies, the kind of day that makes being a Lollipop Lady to be envied, I strolled on to the supermarket after my first patrol of the day. Halfway along the main road there was another Lollipop person, a man of about sixty. I paused to chat and compare notes. Whereas I was enjoying being admired by ogling motorists and bread delivery men, Tom found his part-time job ideal for chatting up young office girls and pretty young married women. Indeed, Tom had a glint in his eye all the time he talked, and even tried his hand at chatting me up! He was in jovial, wise-cracking mood.

'Headmistress down at Junior School's leaving at Easter,' he told me. 'Ah've 'ad an invitation to attend her farewell party at school on the 23rd. Suppose you'll be getting one as well. Wonder if she'll fancy playing Postman's Knock, or owt like that?'

I declined Tom's offer of a practice run there and then. He went on, 'I remember the first time I went down to school for my free midday dinner.' (I could have availed myself of that too, but not much use when my children refused to stay.) 'I sees this posh, grey-haired woman breezing along the corridor,' Tom recalled, twiddling his pole faster and faster as he gleefully told his initial encounter with the retiring headmistress. 'She stalked up to me as I stood hanging about wondering where ah't to go for t'free do.'

'Then what?' I asked.

'"Well my man, what do you want?"' Tom's eyes glittered with laughter, and tears rolled down his weather-beaten face. 'Naturally, I thought she was one of them there dinner ladies, so I pinched her behind and asked, "What have yer got, luv?"'

'Do you still have your dinners there, Tom?' I asked.

'No, I have a sandwich at the back o' t'dry cleaners, and a swig o' tea from me flask. Ah didn't fancy being under her eagle eye every flipping day.'

I was always glad when Tuesday mornings were over. Elizabeth had her violin lesson then and spent the time from getting out of bed at seven to leaving home at eight screaming threats because she didn't get on with her new teacher. My job on the crossing required all my concentration at times, and I didn't need the nagging thought at the back of my mind that my own child's last words had been, 'I'll strangle myself at school – with the violin string if I can't find anything else!'

But there were advantages to going out to a job, too. Once the morning hurdle of getting one's own family off the premises was over, it was reassuring to listen to the problems of others. Instead of worrying at home, by a quarter to nine the brisk morning air and talking to others made me quite forget my own situation. And when I did remember, my difficulties were seen in perspective. Compared to what some had to endure, moneylenders and supposing I'd end up with nothing was something we could surmount in time, even if it took years.

Elizabeth, I knew, wouldn't really strangle herself – would she? – simply because her new violin teacher wasn't as pleasant as her former one. Words, after all, are cheap, to be listened to, but not to over-react to. Most people, I find, use them a great deal to try and get their own way.

Other mothers had children equally as aggravating – for instance, the capers Brown Grandad's granddaughter got up to. I secretly called him Brown Grandad because winter, spring, summer and autumn alike, he forever wore the same shapeless, brown check suit, with an old-fashioned 'Albert' on a gold chain, dangling across his comfortable-looking tummy. He wore the kind of spectacles that appear to be cut in half, and peered belligerently over the top of them all the time. But there was a lurking twinkle in his eyes as well.

I enjoyed seeing Brown Grandad shambling like a big bear down the lane on school mornings. A typical grandad – the more Beverley teased, the more he loved it, while putting on an exaggerated show of being the Stern Disciplinarian. The format was the same, day after day. No matter how firmly Brown Grandad held his granddaughter's hand in his own gnarled one (a hand with brown age spots to match his suit), the little girl was a veritable Houdini. Before he could blink a faded eyelash she'd slipped his hoary, all-enveloping fist and danced off giggling to the edge of the pavement.

'Little – so and so!' he growled as he grinned broadly at me, and clenched his fist into a boxer's. 'Hey – come here, you young devil!' he hollered, red cheeks puffing and pouting, tummy bumping up and down beneath the crumpled brown waistcoat. 'Stop her – stop the so and so!'

But Beverley would never have gone on to the road. I wouldn't have let her, in any case. It was simply her way of showing affection for Brown Grandad, a bit of fun, providing him with a bit of adrenaline to keep him going, and on his slippered toes.

'It's harder than working, by Gad,' he exclaimed to me often. 'I'm fair relieved when I'm off duty, and it's Saturday and Sunday, and her mother's looking after her.'

The fish and chip shop man's wife was glad when weekends came round, too, for every Monday morning the merry-go-round started again. Once Beverley and Brown Grandad had safely crossed the road they headed for the snicket between Nellie's grocer shop and the wet-fish shop, which was a short cut to school. Mrs Robinson, the fish and chip shop man's wife, had to hang her smalls in the gloomy bit of space between the shops; at the other side was Miss Jones, the draper. Occasionally a couple of Mr Robinson's work shirts were blowing on the line as well. (Often clothes, like pets, resemble the person who owns them. Mr Robinson's shirts were like that. Anything but Savile Row.) Then, helter skelter between the clean washing would zigzag Beverley, with Brown Grandad in hot pursuit. It was hide and seek between the flapping clothes, with Brown Grandad every now and again zooming into view between the fish and chip shop's ballooning Sunday knickers and Y-fronts. An outraged face would appear for a split second between a gusset, while Beverley sang, 'Can't catch me for a Big Fat Bear, Grandad!' Eventually, caught at last, captor and captive would saunter hand in hand into the sweet shop, the best of pals.

Sometimes Beverley's other Grandad from the opposite end of town stood in for Brown Grandad, and everyone, including Beverley, was dull and decorous when it was his day. He was a decent enough chap, but one you instinctively knew wasn't to be fooled around with. How boring.

One Monday morning when it was the other Grandad's turn to look after Beverley, I enquired, 'Is the other one having a rest today?'

'Good God, the old boy needs it,' relied the immaculately dressed, lean and much more sophisticated ancestor. He wore a fashionable sheepskin jacket and suede shoes – not the kind to play hide and seek in between a fish shop owner's knickers and underpants. I bet only his wife ever saw him in slippers.

'This little minx makes the poor old boy almost squint-eyed trying to keep one eye on the traffic and the other on her,' sighed Sheepskin, though obviously very much in charge of any situation himself.

Beverley was a real little Jekyll and Hyde; demure smiles and perfect behaviour were the rule of the day when Grandad Sheepskin was in charge, but so lacking in fun.

On the tenth of March, a typically changeable day with wind and rain all morning, there were blue skies as I dashed up our lane to prepare a midday snack. Then in the afternoon the wind howled like a raging tornado against a background of ominous-looking dark grey clouds. In thieving mood the wind tore off my navy beret and whirled it in front of an oncoming trolleybus – more entertainment for the No 73's passengers, all peering out of rain-splattered windows.

An old gentleman raced after the beret, grabbed the muddy object and handed it back to me.

'Don't think that'll do much for you at Ascot, lass,' he said.

As with any uniform, however humble, it must be worn properly, and the sodden beret did little to enhance my already windswept appearance. But with hair wet through and bedraggled I plonked it back on my head, looking more like somebody from a Laurel and Hardy film than the sex symbol of the main road crossing I used to pretend I was at one time.

On such gale-force days I was more like a lion-tamer – the wild animal being the crossing pole. It lurched this way and that, groaned and pushed its leering face up against those defenceless pedestrians unlucky enough to be on the crossing with a crowd of schoolchildren and me. That pole sent many a hat skimming off heads, and, taking a bow, laddered many nylons, to say nothing of a sudden swoop lifting a skirt when completely out of my control.

'Oh, I'm so sorry,' I said scores of times on windy days when a gust suddenly wrenched the pole from its upright position and cracked somebody on the head.

'It's all right, Lollipop, not your fault – this bloody wind,' was the usual rueful response.

On the credit side, such a day did fill lungs with fresh air, great gusts of it, and swept away any spiders than might still be lurking after the long winter. Above all, on a day like that it made me feel alive, and even able to face the products of Elizabeth's Domestic Science lesson. I've gone home to apple crumble with pastry more like a slab of cement and sponge cake that a crane would have difficulty lifting. Eating that lot before going on duty would surely have anchored me firmly to the ground.

4

Hope springs eternal

*H*eavy rain and winds necessitated a bathnight for the Lollipop plastic-type coat. It became filthy, certainly not the dazzling stop-the-traffic white that a motorist ideally should be able to see a mile off.

'Scrub it with Vim,' warned Tom the warden up the road on the other crossing, when I'd mentioned using that, 'and it'll lose its waterproofing. Elbow grease is best.'

But the dirt was so deeply ingrained after a bad day weatherwise that hot water and elbow grease alone were never sufficient. So, on bathnight for the coat my husband was hauled into the bathroom to assist. Armed with two scrubbing brushes and soap, we set to work over every plastic inch. It proved worse than bathing a dog, it slithered and flapped about so much.

We had to make sure of a fine evening so it could be hung outside to dry on the line. But that also meant having to treat mother for shock when she came round the back in the dusk and saw a couple of outstretched, stiff white arms facing her! A drop of brandy was administered, courtesy of the pub Granville was currently being a waiter for most evenings, and weekends as well, to try and keep pace with the moneylenders' demands. His ordinary daytime job, plus my Lollipop wages and the evening jobs, were never enough. It was like King Canute vainly trying to hold back the oncoming tide.

A Hungarian lady who had come to live further up the lane after the trouble in her country was also in an awful state of 'nerves' one morning as she frantically beckoned to me when she spotted me returning after the first crossing of the day.

'Hazel, can I talk to you a minute? I don't know what the milkman will think. You see, I practise yoga, and I quite forgot it was his day to call for the money. There I was, in my pants and vest, standing on my head in the living room. I never heard him knock, and as I looked through the window – upside-down – there was this man's face, with his mouth wide open. He didn't knock again. What if he thinks we foreigners are all – well – like *that?*'

I calmed her down by promising to explain to the milkman all about her yoga when I saw him again on the crossing at midday, which I usually did. Inflated with a feeling of even more importance – fancy, not only boss of a main road crossing, but now looked up to by the Public At Large to solve their problems as well! – I went in home for coffee and cat time, with Prince on my knee for a few reassuring cuddles. When I looked in the mirror, what a sight! Two red lipstick stains on both cheeks, making me look like a clown from Blackpool Circus. The Hungarian lady had been so grateful when I promised to explain to the milkman what she'd been up to – or down to – that she had kissed me impulsively. What a good job I'd been on my way home, and not to the crossing.

Next day, 21 March, was the day to move the clocks forward. Previously, this occurrence had been of no significance, not then having had to dress and put make-up on first thing in a morning. But I hardly slept for worrying about being on the crossing an hour earlier. What a responsibility! After all, if I wasn't there on time, and a child was killed or injured because of me not being there with Lollipop…

That Monday morning, the first official day of spring, my stand at the crossing was still in shadow as I appeared at what, the week before, would have been seven thirty. The change-over put me right back into bitterest winter again. My fingers, even in my Large Men's gloves, felt numb with cold as I took hold of the ice-encrusted pole, which, poor thing, had to spend all its nights outside, down the snicket at the side of Nellie's shop.

I kept curling my fingers up inside the gloves, leaving the glove fingers hanging loose, to try and get circulation back into them. Had any Lollipop Lady – or Man – ever had to have fingers amputated because of the intense cold? Standing about, after all, is always much colder than striding out on a brisk walk.

Also, in quite moments, simply standing still all those hours, lifting one foot then another to try and keep warm, I worried about getting varicose veins – then doubts about the job assailed me yet again. Was it worth it? Surely there were better ways of earning a living than standing like a frozen statue while huge hailstones bounced against one's face? Then life came round the corner in the shape of laughing children, and the joy of living took over.

On the evening of the 23rd Tom and I attended the Headmistress's Farewell Party at the Junior School – were they sad or glad, I wondered… A young singing teacher contributed in her sweet, youthful voice to the entertainment, singing 'My Mother Bids me Bind My Hair', and the Headmistress, obviously striving to hold back her tears, thanked everyone – 'Including the two crossing wardens, who bravely man their posts come wind, hail or snow.'

Now it was my turn to hold back my emotions. 'I wonder if we'll be mentioned in next January's Honours List?' I nudged Tom.

'Are yer ruddy joking?' he grinned.

The song about binding hair could have been a hint to me. Never a fan of hairdressers, I wore mine shoulder length, allowing it to go its own naturally, wavy way. Perhaps if I'd been the type to lacquer it down I'd have looked less like one of those Dulux dogs with hair blown all over on stormy days. (Wish I could remember to say Dulux and not Durex when describing that breed…)

On 29 March we awoke to a picturesque blue sky and bright sunshine. But there had been frost during the night, and when I went down the snicket to get Lollipop it felt like a vertical iceberg. However, probably as a result of longer daylight and more sunshine, everyone now walked with a spring in their step. Even the old straightened up more to greet the brighter days, and the local men jauntily tripped across the road to Nellie's for their packet of fags and newspaper, having first bared sometimes hairy chests to the early morning air (the hairy-chested ones risking the air sooner than the unhairy).

I saw lots of V-shaped hairy male chests before nine o'clock. Most I greeted with a cheerful 'Morning, Tarzan'. Some gave a quick squeeze, and occasionally a fleeting kiss if nobody was looking who might report back to 'their missus'.

Oh, glorious! The weather had been worth waiting for. I was glad that I hadn't given in to the bad weather temptations to pack the job in. Now were the beginnings of really pleasurable days in the open air. Caroline and the other schoolchildren dispensed with heavy winter duffle coats, blossoming out in blazers, pretty dresses and sandals. Of course there were still the occasional setbacks to the weather, but we were climbing up the mountain of the year, not going down it. It was good to stand back against the now warm wall, with Lollipop, who now felt to be a real friend, almost another person by my side.

I watched cosseted dogs, tongues dripping drops of saliva on to their owner-driver's shoulder, like leaking lavatory cisterns. Sometimes they rested their furry heads on the drivers' shoulders, taking it easy in the back seat while creating a race of lob-sided motorists, especially if it was a heavy breed of dog. I was glad they hadn't been left bored stiff in a house all day long. Those who did leave dogs made me furious when they said, 'Oh, but he/she has a marvellous bladder.' Hobson's Choice isn't it, if you have nowhere to go…

Easter. Resurrection. The hope of better things to come. Even at our house, beset with money problems as we were, hope still sprang eternal.

I'd always encouraged Elizabeth and Caroline to observe life and to keep a diary, preferably seeing the funny side, because however gloomy the outlook, there always is one. I was therefore thrilled that both children were to have their talks – 'Funny Faces' by Elizabeth, and 'A Long Time Till Morning' by Caroline – broadcast on the *Northern Drift* programme, and we splashed out and bought a wireless. It cost fifteen guineas, which had to be paid by the end of June to get it at cost price. But even if it meant we were turned out of the house, I wasn't going to miss hearing our daughters actually broadcasting – and besides, like Mr Micawber, I kidded myself that something was bound to turn up before anything that drastic.

Perhaps I could try sending a talk about life on a school crossing, then what I earned with that could pay for the wireless – if only I had more time. What with going up and down that lane four times a day, baking to try and fill hungry stomachs (cheaper than bought stuff), shopping, housework, sending letters to magazines in the hope of a guinea or two – keeping busy kept me from despair, while threatening letters and bills came in with far more regularity than cheques.

I'd have more time when we broke up for the Easter holidays, but only half pay. But breaking up on 30 March was quite a wrench. By then I had come to think of the crossing as my own private property, and couldn't imagine life continuing without me to direct proceedings. And how about my subjects? Workers, children, John the gardener, Tom the warden, old people who relied on me for somebody to talk to in their widowed loneliness – and the motorists who tooted their horns in cheery greetings every day? However, I tried to look on the bright side. The break would give me the opportunity to catch up with home dust rather than road dust. Nevertheless, I was really going to miss my daily doses of fresh air, being paid for it, and the easy comradeship of people who daily used that portion of the main road.

On the last morning before the Easter break began I took fish and chips up for midday dinner with Caroline. For tea, having no money left, we just had potatoes in jackets, then rice pudding for tea. Panic set it.

'Wish I was married to a husband who could provide proper blasted meals,' I stormed apologetically as I plonked the meagre meal on plates. I spent the evening knitting – another occupation to make things instead of having to buy them. It took time, but also made me know I wasn't wasting it.

Then I calmed down, looking back on the interview I had with a young couple that week, both in wheelchairs, but optimistically getting married – Maureen in full white wedding dress and veil. I sold the piece to the local newspaper. Gosh, how lucky we were really, being able to walk. Even though we hadn't a car to zoom around in, we could *walk*. What would they give for that, Maureen and her brave husband?

At least this was the first time ever I'd been paid for something I wasn't doing – thirty shillings a week during school holidays. How enjoyable collecting it every Thursday morning. At least it made me feel able to buy ice-creams for Elizabeth and Caroline as we dashed into cafés to shelter from Easter downpours – and to buy brandy snap, and a singing bird toy for Prince, which we bought from the fair. How Prince enjoyed leaping up after that bright green paper bird on the end of a stick, the children whirling it high in the air while eager tabby paws reached to catch it! A back garden on a spring day and a singing paper bird can constitute a cat's paradise, after a winter of cosy content.

The Authors' Circle, of which I was a member, was due to meet at our house on the evening of 4 April. I moved all the furniture in the front room to one side in order to vac the carpet, but the old vacuum cleaner just puffed out dust, and when I asked Caroline to shake her duster, she did. In the middle of the room.

Bartering became a way of life when 'up against it'. I was delighted when, having to buy shoes, I noticed that the binding was a bit loose, and got 9s 11d knocked off as a result. Cabbage, raw from the garden, was a useful standby as a basis for salad instead of buying lettuce, and with tomatoes and hard-boiled eggs it often 'kept body and soul together', as mother was fond of saying. At least the cabbage had no additives, apart from the odd slug.

I cried a little on 10 April, my 39th birthday, because birthdays after childhood are nothing to celebrate, only a resounding tolling of the Bells of Time. I never thought the time would really come when I only had one more year to go till forty – twenty sounds so much better! Granville gave me stockings, a jar of cold cream, and a ten shilling note. Where he'd managed to get that from he didn't say – maybe a tip from a customer at the Fleece. Caroline gave me a purse and a swinging dwarf for the garden, Elizabeth a bunch of pink tulips, and Tweed perfume. Mother and my stepfather give them spending money, or they'd never have been able to give anything.

The next day, Easter Monday, Granville took the girls to the fair. I stayed at home, catching up on various jobs, and prepared big baked potatoes in the gas oven and a huge rice pudding for their return. Then there was celebration next morning, with the prize of a tea caddy full of tea for a letter of mine published in *The People's Friend* – so no need to buy tea for some time.

It was snowing on the 14th, and when we went to collect my retaining wage we were too late, so would have to wait till next week – what a blow. Next day a friend phoned to say the weather was too bad to visit, snowing heavily. We spent time looking up words in the dictionary. Elizabeth didn't know the word for 'sewage works', and I said by mistake it was 'suet works' – it was one way to make our own amusements than paying to go to a show.

On the last day of the Easter holidays I had to draw both Elizabeth's and Caroline's money out of their bank, and my own, agreeing to pay them back with two shillings interest each, when I was paid. I'm sure it's more exciting to shop with limited means than with money galore. I bought pyjamas for Granville for 29s 11d (you can't sleep in the nude in an unheated bedroom when snow is piling up on the windowsill outside), a suspender belt for me at 12s 11d, a bra for 19s 11d, and a much-needed new shirt for Granville, 17s 11d, followed by the treat of lunch in a café, it being the last day of the holidays.

We watched *Play of the Week* on television and Granville went 'waiting on' at the Fleece. Caroline was crying in bed later because she didn't want to go back to school the following day. So the holidays came to an end, after lazy mornings staying in bed later than usual, long walks in the countryside, gathering palms to fill the tall vases, and occasionally fighting off the usual onslaught of gentlemen who came to the door enquiring why such and such a bill hadn't yet been paid. I had no idea – except that there wasn't money to pay them with. But if a cheque for a guinea came in the post, for a letter of mine published in a magazine, we all did a war dance of delight. We'd win through yet!

5

Sweet charity

Contrariwise, when the day came to begin at the crossing once more, I felt a pang of regret at having to keep to a timetable again. But it soon wore off. Everyone slipped into their usual routine. So did the weather. The rain beat down on me unceasingly as I went across the main road and down the snicket to be reunited with Lollipop at eight thirty. But there must be something in the saying that 'rain is good for the complexion' because a postman began paying me compliments.

'How about coming to t'pictures with me one evening, Hazel? Your husband needn't find out. I think you're smashing! Say you're going with a friend.'

I wasn't even tempted. He was small, with owl-like eyes behind similar specs. Someone to escape from, not make an excuse to be with.

'Oh, I'm sorry, but I'm far too busy,' I replied. 'Besides, it isn't fair on your wife, is it?'

But it was good for my ego to be asked. I suppose that even on pelting-down-with-rain mornings, even a middle-aged postman's thoughts will often turn to love. Or lust. I didn't want to find out which. He wasn't that swashbuckling policeman... Even the bright-eyed young new Indian teacher from the Junior School lost his shyness when it came to spring, and talked to me about his homeland, and about writing.

'I love writing poetry,' he told me. 'I could write one about you if you like...' There can even be culture on the crossing at times!

The Indian teacher always looked smart in his dark suit and black overcoat. Such encounters took my mind off our money problems – having to go to town on the bus after the first crossing to meet Granville, and borrow £8 from Lloyds Bank to allow us to manage until next pay day.

Sadly, springtime only signified spring cleaning and ill health for some of the old ladies I talked to on the crossing. Mrs Jackson, in her eighties, lived in the council bungalows not far from the crossing. Her skin was drawn tightly over her bird-like features, wrinkled deeply like yellowing parchment. Most days she hobbled up to me, leaning heavily on her walking stick, for someone to talk to.

'I can't get shut of this blessed indigestion,' she complained one morning, her face narrower and yellower-looking than usual. 'But they won't get me to that there doctor o' mine, no fear. He'd have me whipped into hospital and x-rayed soon as look at me.' Mrs Jackson stood very near to me, being hard of hearing. She smelled of faded mothballs and stale lavender water. But I felt sorry for the old widow, and liked her. She had a captive audience with me when I wasn't taking children across the road; a listening ear is something many lonely old people miss.

'Ah couldn't sleep in the night,' she continued, 'so ah got up about four and started cleaning me kitchen cupboard out. Ah came across an old packet of Morlands, thought they might steady me gall gladder. 'Ere, 'ave one.'

Before I could back away a bony finger and thumb had pushed one into my mouth. I was truly speechless.

'I'm a devil for nuts as well, Hazel' laughed Mrs Jackson, leaning more heavily on one side before shifting her slight frame to the other. 'Peanuts, monkey nuts, Brazil nuts – you name 'em, ah've got 'em. Or at least I did have till I saw a few spiders and other stuff crawling on 'em at back o' t'cupboard. So ah shut me eyes and flung 'em all on t'fire back. Ah'm sucking Morlands now instead.'

When taken unawares before, I'd had the sense to say 'Thank you, I'll keep them for when I'm not working,' and put the suspicious-looking objects in my coat pocket, to be thrown on our fire later. But Mrs Jackson wasn't easily put off.

'See lass, here's another to put in thi pocket.' She grovelled into the packet again, extricating another white pellet. 'Well, ah'll be off to t'chemist then now, missus. Get mesen a bottle of glycerine and olive oil. If that doesn't dissolve me stones, nowt will. That reminds me (as a bread van flew past), it's me bread day. Two small loaves last me a week. You'll find you don't eat so much when you get older, missus.' (I was 'missus' when she momentarily forgot my name.)

After seeing Mrs Jackson safely on her way I considered her remark about not eating so much as one became older. Someone in my position, with 'finance companies', or whatever fancy names those who preyed on the vulnerable gave themselves, also don't eat much at times.

Those sombre misgivings were driven out of my mind when the Eternal Schoolgirl – as I thought of the Down's syndrome lady – came tripping up to me. Immediately my own situation became wonderful compared to hers. Fifty if she was a day, Mary still dressed as a schoolgirl and affected similar mannerisms. Even before she was anywhere near me her hand was held out beseechingly, eager for the moment when I accepted it and my hand closed over her podgy one. Her straight, mousy-coloured hair was parted at the side and tied with a pink ribbon bow.

'Take me across, Mrs Wheeler,' commanded little Miss Fussy Breeches.

That morning, the weather being all baby blue skies with white clouds and the warm scent of newly mown grass from gardens on the breeze, Mary was wearing her scarlet blazer with anonymous badge instead of her winter duffle coat.

'You're looking very smart this morning, Mary,' I said, as we set off to the middle of the crossing. Her wide face wrinkled into a smile of delight.

'Do you like my skirt, too, Mrs Wheeler?'

Childlike, she pirouetted in front of me a couple of times, holding out the white pleated garment, gazing at me for approval. Short white ankle socks and black low-heeled buttoned shoes completed her Bessie Bunter-like ensemble, not forgetting her brown satchel, which she used instead of a shopping basket.

I felt slightly eerie when with Mary, as if she was a character from a schoolgirl paper of the 'thirties come to life. But I knew that she'd never change even if we were both meeting on the crossing fifty years ahead. Nature had trapped Mary for ever. Circumstances alone had trapped me. But only for the time being. Escape was possible. Once again, a lowly Lollipop Lady as I appeared to all, I stood there and counted my blessings. This was an acceptance, coupled with determination, that I'd never have come round to had I been in the house alone, waiting for another lot of bills to come through the letterbox.

I never found out where Mary went to all day, or who she lived with. A first I felt a little repelled by the thick damp, clammy hand in mine. But there was no escaping her grip. It was like a vice. And although it was legally against the rules to take anyone across the road except schoolchildren, Mary was in far greater need of assistance than many of the older, brighter children.

It was the same with aged, infirm or blind people. One afternoon I had to attend instructions about being a crossing warden, together with the town's other Lollipop team, while policemen manned the crossings. One of the rules emphatically stated that no warden was empowered to help anyone other than schoolchildren across a road. The wording on the poles said it all: 'STOP – CHILDREN CROSSING'. It meant exactly what it said, we were told.

It's a different matter, however, sitting in an office making rules and regulations to having to carry them out to the letter on the roads outside. Twice daily a practically blind eight-two-year-old lady timed herself to set off for the Workshop for the Blind when she knew that I would be on duty. How could I say to her, if no other adult was around to offer to take her arm and walk her across the main road, 'I'm sorry, but I'm not allowed to take you across'? Maybe she'd miss her bus too, and have to wait in the draughty shelter until another came.

Mrs Sanderson always carried a bag of striped humbugs – and the first time I encountered her she pushed one into my mouth, feeling about with thin fingers until she had located it correctly. It was a kind of 'Thank you' gesture, as one might give a biscuit to a dog for being a good boy. Or girl.

I had to explain that it was dangerous for me to have a huge boiled sweet in my mouth when working. I could choke if there was a sudden crisis and I forgot it was there. Mrs Sanderson looked crestfallen. A humbug a day was her guarantee to have the Lollipop Lady on her side.

But quite apart from the possibility of choking, I've always cleaned my teeth after eating, and certainly didn't want to have false ones from a surfeit of humbugs and other sweets administered on the school crossing. Should I start bringing toothbrush, bottle of water and my tube of Euthymol with me? I'd rather have my own teeth than a big bank balance any day.

Yet old people can be touchy, even mortally offended, if an offering is declined. They are brought up not wanting to accept charity, but to pay for services given, as far as they are able. Unlike in ordinary circumstances, being able to run away when someone approaches that you don't want to see, it's impossible when on the job.

Next day Mrs Sanderson had forgotten about my saying I couldn't eat sweets on duty. So it had to be gone through all over again. Apart from looking after my teeth, I didn't want to be seen by the gorgeous policeman with one cheek bulging with a monster striped humbug. A hurt expression distorted her aged face beneath her green felt hat.

'Surely you can't dislike *humbugs*, Mrs Wheeler? I was brought up on them.'

My heart thumped with dread whenever I heard the tap, tap of her white stick against the bollards on the opposite side of the road. And as I felt her skeleton-like arm beneath the folds of her bottle-green loose tweed coat, I hoped never to live to be almost blind, my life a round of fumbling for food, labouring in a workshop for the blind for a few shillings daily, and my body reduced to a shapeless worn-out workshop itself, all sense of joie de vivre gone from it for ever, never to return – no man ever again to covet it, becoming only a slow moving object of sagging flesh, brittle bones and pursed-up mouth.

I was both relieved and glad that those I escorted across the road couldn't read my thoughts, hoping that a bus, or anything, would bring a merciful end to my life before it degenerated into some such shamble. But I had a hunch that I'd depart this life if I remained as a Lollipop Lady, not by being run over, by disease or drowning, but by somebody cramming a huge boiled sweet into my gob when I wasn't looking. (I don't usually say 'gob', but it *did* fit the situation.)

Besides Mrs Sanderson, some elderly men were also apparently convinced that the way to a Lollipop Lady's heart was by plying her with tobacco-soiled hard-boiled sweets from the depths of their trouser pockets, or screwed-up toffees in wrinkled, ancient paper. These were usually Riley's toffee rolls, which, I must admit, I find damned hard to resist. Especially if they've gone a bit soft and squashy.

One near-death experience happened on the crossing when such a gift was in my mouth. A cluster of children were being a bit unruly, and forgetting about the toffee in my mouth, I yelled for them to come 'Right across' – and narrowly missed being asphyxiated as the monstrosity in my mouth slid to the back of my throat.

6

Raining, cats and dogs

A tiny pup from up the lane stealthily followed its next-door neighbour whenever she set off for town. Only when she stopped by me to wait for the bus was Bingo seen, leaping up at her skirt in effusive delight. When shooing Bingo back home had not the slightest effect and a bus was coming, she scooped the puppy up and handed him to me.

'Here Hazel – you'll have to have him. My bus is here, I can't be late. He isn't my responsibility. He does this every damned day.'

That was another person I dreaded seeing, and the slyly wagging tail bringing up the rear! It was always such a performance getting Bingo back to safe territory again. One morning, concerned as usual for the bright-eyed puppy's welfare, and stuck with him in my arms as well as Lollipop, I in turn handed Bingo into the arms of another, who agreed to take him back home.

'I'm not going to town, only shopping locally, but you'll have to look after him until I go back home and lock our Whiskers in the front room,' she gabbled. 'Our Whiskers'll go hell for leather at poor old Bingo if she sees him.' She looked round her frantically as children came up, and loads of traffic. 'Ee, it's a bit of a devil for you, isn't it, Hazel, no dog lead or anything.'

I could have replied that the Education Department didn't supply those to their Lollipop people, but I did wonder whether I should buy one and bring it to the crossing with me every day for such predicaments. Those pet owners who don't leave their so-called 'pets' outside all day to be a danger to themselves and others, but neglect to keep them safe inside their own gardens, are also at fault. It must be particularly distressing for imprisoned animals in houses as well as cats during the long hot days of summer, though it's not as much penance to be indoors all day when winter blizzards blow. But it's equally boring for an animal that, ideally, should be walking in woods and fields when the summer sun is shining. What mental torment to see the sun outside, and not able to be part of the summer scene but cooped up inside a house or flat.

But even the most perfect midsummer day brings pain, if not outright tragedy, to some. As I sauntered down the lane to the crossing one lovely June afternoon, wearing my white cotton summer Lollipop coat on the last stint of the day, my heart beat faster at sight of a crowd where I stood, and the policeman taking notes.

Two cars had collided, the front one right where I stood on pausing in the middle of the road before continuing right across. Before the first of the Infant School came dancing up out of the snicket or up the road I had time to talk with the occupant of the first car. He bent his head, ferreting among his hair. Parting the lank greasy stuff, he pointed.

'Bleeding, isn't it?'

'Yes, it is,' I agreed, shivering involuntarily as the rapidly congealing dark blood spilled over the hair parting.

It was some time before the sightseers, officials and wounded departed. At such times one appreciates more than ever the necessity for someone to see little ones across busy roads. A second earlier and one of the infants may have come out of school early, darted across the road without going to the crossing, and been injured.

Since becoming one of the 'Lollipop People' I avidly read anything about them. In the evening paper there was a letter ridiculing allowing inexperienced old age pensions to have such a responsible job. But surely an intelligent, physically active older person in charge is better than nobody at all.

Next day, fame at last! A reporter from the local paper telephoned. Could he come and talk to me about what it was like being a Lollipop Lady? The handsome young reporter and I drank coffee and enjoyed home-made scones as we talked when I came back after the first crossing of the day.

'Being a crossing warden is not a job for an old, old age pensioner,' I said. 'Nor for a person without much intelligence, despite a Lollipop Person's lowly image. One has to be alert, and ready for all manner of unexpected happenings on the job. Being a Lollipop Lady – or Man – is more of a calling, like a doctor,' I laughed. 'But not something anyone would do for the money alone. It certainly isn't worth all the buffeting about in all weathers for less than four pounds a week.' But, as I told him, it was ideal for me – only a walk to the crossing at the end of our lane. And I always preferred to take the children to school myself, even when the warden was on duty before I took the job over.

While it was still daylight for ages after the children came home from school, more disputes erupted with neighbours than any uproar on the crossing. When tennis balls spun dizzily over our garden fence, narrowly missing windows, it was a far more hazardous occupation being a mother than a Lollipop Lady. After yet another ball had become lost and we hadn't dared ask for it back, I set the alarm clock for five in the morning in order to sneak into next door's garden and retrieve it. Feeling like a heroine out of *Peg's Own Paper*, I rose at the crack of dawn and was shocked to discover a tent with gently snoring humans on next door's immaculate lawn.

Hardly daring to breathe, let alone snore, I crept round the tent and eventually found the lost tennis ball. I longed for a time when Elizabeth and Caroline had other interests – or even for winter to return – to stop having to carry on like a cat burglar every so often.

Such thoughts were idly crossing my mind on the long hazy last day of June after escorting Andrew and Debbie to the opposite side of the road when there was a tap on my shoulder. It was almost half past one. I could hear the school bell, and I didn't want to waste time talking when I could be dashing up home.

'Cross my palm with silver, dearie, and I'll tell your fortune.'

I turned and met the intense, dark-eyed gaze of a gypsy, her eyes smouldering in the midday heat.

'I'm sorry, but I haven't any with me,' I replied. 'And it's time for me to go off duty now.' The gypsy held my arm.

'Never mind the silver then, dearie, but I'll tell you summat for nowt. I see a baby boy – you're going to have a baby boy. Before the year's out as well.'

I stared at her, clutching Lollipop like a petrified snake.

'That isn't all either. You'll not end your days in the house you're in now.'

Rosy visions of a calmer future shattered that gorgeous June afternoon, my mind as agitated as if war had been declared. The lovely day that, moments ago, had felt timeless and ageless, with the sense that life could only get better, evaporated. Looking ahead to a time when the moneylenders might be paid off and the children more independent now lay in ruins at my feet. What a prospect, to be hopelessly bowed down with baby routine again, no chance to even earn the bit of money I did as a Lollipop Lady. Were we to end up in the workhouse – if such places still existed? I felt sick.

The gypsy grinned malevolently.

'P'raps you'll show me your little lad, next time I'm round here.'

Then off she shuffled on laceless black pumps up the dusty main road in search of her next victim.

A light-hearted prance down the snicket to garage Lollipop had turned my day into a heavy problem. A baby before the end of the year? I counted on my fingers. July, August, September, October – four months – November, December – only six months. To the best of my knowledge all that my anatomy contained was the usual organs, yet I could not rid myself of the mental pictures of having to say goodbye to this existence of fresh air, nappyless days, and nights of undisturbed sleep. Drat the woman! She was a fool! And yet – they can put curses on people, can't they? And I hadn't crossed her palm with silver…

Instead of whizzing through the bedrooms with vac and duster as planned, I moped away the couple of hours before leaving for the crossing again, searching the pages of my diary, working out what month it would be, nine from now. I browsed through a copy of *Every Woman's Enquire Within*, hoping to eradicate morbid thoughts about gypsy spells and virgin births. And with Granville working in pubs every night, neither of us had much inclination for passion.

Then I pondered how I'd reveal the fact of a baby brother's imminence to Elizabeth and Caroline – and what on earth would mother say? She who, each time she had been told of my pregnancy, had assumed an expression of doom and intoned, 'Oh, I do wish it was all over!'

No, it simply did not bear thinking about. So I had a quick sherry (a bottle lasted ages, and was only used in emergencies) then set off to talk with people on the crossing, and ask them if they had experienced any gypsy's warnings coming true.

My mind wasn't concentrating a hundred per cent on my work that session. Crikey, I'd be almost forty-nine before the baby was ten. I'd look a real old hag trailing it down to the crossing in ten years' time. God, next time I saw a gypsy ambling towards me I'd make sure I could either cross her hand with silver, or have a pair of ear-plugs handy.

The night was punctuated with restlessness and questions. 'Would you like to have a boy?' I nudged the tattered blue and white striped pyjamas again and again. 'How could we afford one, when we can barely afford to feed the four of us now, and still pay money into court every week, and all the other blasted commitments?'

'Stop nattering and get to sleep,' was his sleepy response. 'You're not having a baby – not mine anyway. So shurrup.'

But I continued. I really felt that once again the Fates were against me. We might have had intercourse in our sleep one night, not realising. Did he think that possible?

'Not how I've been lately,' was his laconic response before his snoring took over.

'But she *said* so, a baby boy…' Then I too drifted off to dreamland. All the anguish that encounter caused, all for nothing, the moral being, 'Don't take everything you are told, even by a gypsy, as Gospel.' Listen to what others say, for entertainment, by all means, but don't lose any sleep or buy crates of gin and pennyroyal to try and effect a miscarriage just because a glib-tongued gypsy crosses your path.

The day after my encounter with the gypsy fortune-teller I was in deep conversation with a neighbour's wife who had recently had a second son. I had even reached the point where a name had been decided for mine. Philip Adrian – Philip after my brother. I had even prematurely invited the neighbour's new little boy to Philip Adrian's first birthday party!

For a few days I was fascinated talking to Mrs Schofield, and learning the differences to expect between girl and boy babies. Even when it all became clear that the gypsy had been spouting a load of hot air, my relationship with Mrs Schofield was the teeniest, weeniest bit clouded because of poor Philip Adrian, who never put in an appearance after all. I stopped looking into prams containing baby girls, secretly wondering, 'Will you be my daughter-in-law, maybe in 1990 or thereabouts?' What unnecessary panics we endure because of taking notice of everything we are told!

The first few days of July passed cold and grey, with only thoughts of summer to come (not holidays – we couldn't afford any) and every day my own to do with as I pleased to keep me going. I enjoy winter up to a point if it *is* winter, and seasonable with it. But a grey cold summer is a No Man's Land.

By the 10th we all were thinking that the unseasonable weather was bound to alter soon. I stood holding Lollipop, racking my brains as to where we could take the children for a day out. Maybe we'd manage a day at Chester Zoo. It wouldn't cost too much on the bus, and it would be a pleasant change to stare at some animals instead of being stared at myself.

So that's where we went, and Heavens, how it rained! The sky went mad. How I longed for my wellingtons and white warden waterproof. We ate sandwiches on the bus, the original idea being to give me more time to photograph the animals in what we had hoped would be the glorious sunshine of a summer day. Then, in due course, one of my animal photographs could be entered in a Photographic Competition, and, still an optimist, win first prize, with which we could wipe out all our debts and begin to live happily ever after – all from the strength of an expression captured on a monkey's face ... or pink posterior. All manner of ideas – including a novelty curtain design – crowded my mind, as means of extricating ourselves from the clutches of those moneylenders. Thinking up captions even before I'd taken the photographs.

However, even the animals were greatly displeased with the torrential downpour. One of the apes shook its fist at me angrily, as though yelling, 'On yer way, Nosey Parkers!' I didn't take a single snap, not wanting to waste an exposure on such a dark day. Maybe there'd be an opportunity for a day at the seaside after we broke up properly.

However, heavy clouds persisted next day, Monday, on the crossing. Housewives moaned, 'What a washday. Have you got yours dry yet?' Before the onset of up-to-date automatic machines, including dryers,

Monday was the favourite day for washing and 'hanging out'. I did our washing when it needed it, not because it was Monday.

The next day was windy as well as raining. On Wednesday torrential rain almost drowned me, stopping abruptly when I entered the house.

So July continued with little change. On the cold, overcast 18th I arrived at the crossing feeling a big grumpy, then saw a couple of men picking up Ginger, one of the cats that, for all too brief a period, had lived in one of the main road semis. They wrapped it in a copy of *The News of the World* and drove off with him in their lorry. What an ignominious end.

'We'll get another,' said the cat's owner, nonchalantly, as the lorry disappeared down the road. How I longed to say, 'Don't be such a damned fool, having a cat on a busy main road.' Such animals haven't 'a cat in Hell's chance', as they say. Whether Prince, our cat, was in mourning I don't know – whether news passed along the cats' grapevine along the main road, then up our lane, about poor Ginger's demise, no one could tell. But for a few days Prince moped about, not eating, not even wanting someone to partner her in a ping-pong game, banging the little ball from wall to wall.

I was thinking about how to get her to the PDSA, and showing my sympathy by tucking a black scarf into the neckline of my Lollipop coat as a mark of respect, when Prince pulled herself together and decided it was still summer, even though the sun refused to shine. Next morning she demanded food, lots of it, then stalked into the wilderness of our back garden to hunt.

7

Holiday blues

*T*here's one benefit about working outside, whether the sun shines or not: even the palest, most insipid-looking person acquires some healthy glow of the skin after a few weeks. I felt deeply gratified when, rushing to put Lollipop away after first duty, a passing greengrocer bellowed from his van, 'Hey, Lollipop, you've got a smashing tan. I could take you out given the chance!'

Wow! Doesn't the heat catch you unaware when at last it does arrive? It was quite chilly on the crossing on 21 July first duty, then suddenly the clouds parted and the sun blazed down, cleaving a huge chunk of blue through the grey. Next we knew, all of us were sweltering on one of the hottest days of the year. That tea-time we broke up for the long summer holidays. The crossing looked exactly the same, and so did the schoolchildren, yet the atmosphere had subtly changed. We were all thinking of sand, sea, sunshine and holidays, and here we were, right at the beginning of a whole six weeks of it. Nobody scowled for the rest of the day. None of the boys picked a fight. Smiles wreathed every face, even the teachers.

But I found it difficult to stop my face crumpling into tears when I saw the three little girls whose dad was desperately ill coming towards me. Poor little beggars – it was useless asking them where they were going for their summer holidays. They'd carry on the same as usual, the oldest girl helping her mother clean the small terraced house, blackened by the smoke from neighbouring mill chimneys. They'd go errands to the shops, play in their back yard with their few toys, or sit on walls reading comics passed on to them from friends.

I wondered about inviting them for tea one afternoon. They were pleasant, well-mannered children, lacking the bombast and aggression of some of their 'better off' friends. Whatever simple diversions they found, I fervently hoped they would enjoy the break from school.

Elizabeth had already enjoyed a holiday at the seaside with Grandma and Grandad. The previous weekend she had staggered up the lane from the bus stop weighted down with parcels, refusing to allow anyone to help with her precious load.

The Great Present Opening Ceremony occurred one minute after arriving. The big parcel was for us to share: we unwrapped a huge, cheap-looking dartboard, complete with set of lethal-looking darts.

'I won it with Grandad at Bingo,' she proudly announced. My heart sank. Trust my stepfather to introduce her to Bingo. Now it was a case of God help the cat if darts winged their way across the room. How quickly could we get rid of it...? An idea: 'I say, Elizabeth, bet you'll be able to sell it to a second-hand shop for fifteen shillings.'

Tears welled up in the blue eyes, as she prostrated herself across the dartboard. 'I know you don't like my presents, I know you don't,' she sobbed.

'But I do, the charm bracelet is beautiful.' (If you like mass-produced elephants and hearts clinging to the wrist, straight from Cleethorpes Woolworth's!)

Caroline only needed a wind to use her new kite, and the key-ring for Dad would be useful if he lost the other five.

Knowing the disaster-prone nature of our family, it was the presence of the dartboard that worried me, with visions of trying to extricate darts from Prince's back if they fancied an early morning session, while racing to get to the crossing. The best present of all, of course, was herself, safe and sound at home again.

Even housework can take on the novelty of a holiday when there hasn't been time to tackle jobs properly for weeks. Cleaning all the kitchen shelves on my first day's 'holiday' was most enjoyable, especially listening to talks and a play on the radio at the same time.

Elizabeth and Caroline spent most of the half-crown weekly spending money from Grandad on small toy farm animals and other countryside implements for their toy farm: small plastic green hedges, sixpence each, a farmer bent under the weight of a sack on his back, one and twopence. With toy show-jumpers and their plastic riders, the farm was looking quite impressive. Caroline had received a horse transporter one Christmas, and all the lot lived in that when not being played with. I enjoyed playing with the farmyard as well – it took my mind off reality. One rainy afternoon I spent ages looking through old magazines, cutting out pictures of carrots, onions, apples, pears and other suitable vegetable photographs to fill the tiny wagons. (Reverting to childhood games is far more effective and has no side effects compared with drugs or tranquillisers!) Once we had the farm set up, that Giant from the Big Outside World, Prince, usually yawned, woke up, then stalked all over the assembled figures, indiscriminately knocking everything down.

Every Thursday during the long school summer holidays, Elizabeth, Caroline and I went into town to draw my half pay. It didn't buy much, but there aren't many jobs where a mother can share the same length of holidays as her children.

How bereft my crossing looked, without Lollipop and me. Towards the end of July we had a day in Leeds, hoping to find a suit in the sale, but they were either too big or too small, too cheap looking and tatty or too fabulously elegant – far beyond a Lollipop Lady's pay. So instead I bought a bright red cardigan for 29s 11d, a pair of rubber gloves for washing up, a pan scrub, and a shirt for Granville. Then we treated the farm to a few more horses and pink, curly-tailed little toy pigs. We took afternoon tea in a smart café: tiny triangular sandwiches of mashed-up egg, salad cream and tomatoes, liberally garnished with bright springs of mustard and cress, followed by a plump fresh scone each, smothered in buttercup-yellow butter, and a plate of delicious little cakes, all 'washed down' with hot, refreshing tea poured from a 'silver' teapot.

Then we went home on the train, quite happy with our purchases, and excited about showing Daddy the surprise new shirt bought from my earnings on the crossing – and feeling not at all resentful about the non-existent new suit. It would only have meant having to worry about getting it dirty, and the cost of dry cleaning. Besides, I couldn't afford both, and how wonderful it was to anticipate the delight in Granville's eyes when he was given the shirt – and not yet Christmas! My old tweed suit still had lots of wear in it. It's amazing how, after years of stringent economy, one's mind automatically makes plausible excuses for not getting what was longed for…

On the last Saturday in July, traditionally the week when the local engineering firms and mills closed down for their annual holiday, it rained, and heavily, as it usually did then. So we were glad really that we weren't among the miserable-looking crowds thronging the station and bus queues to escape to the coast.

We went to town. With having to pay out almost everything he earned, what with the mortgage and those other terrible outgoings, Granville had been going to work resembling more of a tramp than an office worker. For once, he was in luck: we saw a pair of lightweight washable men's trousers in a sale. They were only a pound, so I still had enough left from my Lollipop earnings to buy them. We even bought a bit of fresh salmon to accompany the salad for tea, and invited Mrs Broadbent, a widow who lived up the lane, to share it with us as we all watched the football World Cup on television (she hadn't a set of her own).

The rain that pelted down on Sunday washed out July in flood-like conditions. Undeterred, we donned our wellingtons and macs and braved the torrent to walk up the hill to where Tiny, the donkey that belonged to a Children's Home, was in pasture. Tiny wasn't worried about the downpour either. She galloped to meet us, ecstatic when she heard the rustle of paper bags and the orange gleam of a few new carrots. When exotic holidays can't be afforded, children appreciate the pleasures to be enjoyed from the 'simple life'. And there is a lot of pleasure to be had from the sensation of rain on a face devoid of make-up. There were no buses to bother about catching, and how much delight was mutually experienced by giving carrots to a donkey, and having a few words with it! Even donkeys must get bored with their own company sometimes!

'Raining again!' chorused Elizabeth and Caroline as they opened their bedroom window on the first of August.

'Never mind, say White Rabbit for Good Luck, it's the first of the month,' I reminded them. 'Then we'll clear out bedroom drawers and wardrobes. You never know, we might find some forgotten treasure.'

Elizabeth hadn't been chucking things out long before she came across a shoebox full of photographs, taken when they were babies, and often naked. What fun they had laughing uproariously at those snapshots! And there was the satisfaction of tidy drawers and a wardrobe where everything was so much easier to find. Sometimes going away on holiday can be worse than staying at home, and what a gift it is to have whole days to oneself, to do exactly what you want to do. Doesn't cost anything either...

Then next day, at long last, came summer. We went to visit Grandma, who told us she had a 'cold in the nerves'.

The next day summer was over again, and we were re-acquainted with our usual companion, rain. Torrential rain. It was a depressing day, with threatening letters in the post, and trailing round the town in an attempt to pay some of the outstanding bills. What a blessing there were plenty of cabbages in the garden – with grated carrot and raw onion they made a passable salad for lunch.

The rain continued more or less non-stop for eight days. At least I was inside, and not getting soaked through on the crossing. But I was upset for the children. What a let-down of a summer holiday! The novelty of cleaning the house and looking at almost forgotten photographs, with no clock-watching to be at the crossing on time, had worn off. Nerves were beginning to fray, and I began to look forward with eager anticipation to the ordered timetable of being a Lollipop Lady again – and full pay.

But there were still some days to fill. I thought and thought about how I could make the school holiday fun, without having to pay for it.

'Let's take some knitting to the park,' I suggested over-brightly to Elizabeth and Caroline when the sun came out one Monday afternoon.

'*I'm* not – knitting in parks is for old women,' sulked Elizabeth.

How terribly upset I was, not to be able to take them on a proper holiday – and soon the holidays would be over, and so would their childhood... My husband was out every evening working to pay the blasted moneylenders, and what should have been the best years of our lives were blighted. How were we to get through a summer holiday at home with hardly any money?

That evening there was an exhibition of brass-rubbings at a local church. Why not do some ourselves? We had evenings to fill, besides daytimes.

'We could given brass-rubbings as Christmas presents if we started doing them now.' It gave us another idea to fill the interminable hours. But acceptable to whom? Would mother's already overfilled house benefit from being given a huge brass-rubbing of Richard the Lionheart – or whoever it was we brass-rubbed – for a Christmas present? Another idea flagged and died before we bothered to try it.

I was more desperate than ever. I was dealing with atrocious weather, frogs down my wellingtons and speeding motorists on my beloved crossing! Persistent rain and lack of money saps all energy and ideas after a prolonged time. So to stop our energy sapping away completely on the waterlogged 9 August I suggested we have a go at competitions, to try and win what we couldn't afford to buy. A real summer holiday, with sunshine, in the Canary Islands perhaps. Or the Bahamas. Hope springs eternal. We had a batch of entry forms from the supermarket, so concentrated hard for a while, then went to post our entries, coming home to watch the Miss United Kingdom contest on TV. Now, if the children had been a few years older they could have entered that – but wishing wasn't going to get us out of the financial mess we were in. Nor were the odd guineas I kept notching up for letters published in magazines. Nor the pittance I earned as a Lollipop Lady. All those were mere pinpricks against a huge mountainside. So there was nothing for it but to keep plodding on as we were, trying any opportunities that presented themselves to extricate ourselves from an intolerable situation.

Had it not been for the children I often thought I'd have taken the coward's way out and put an end to all the worry. And yet it had all happened because of them – well, because of the toddler next door being allowed to run riot with garden shears and other dangerous stuff. Now we were condemned to spending years of our lives paying for something that should never have been allowed to happen. Neighbours can make or mar another's life – as, indeed, can husbands who can't stand up to them!

But however low and depressed one becomes, invariably a bright spot happens at the lowest ebb to stir up feelings and fading hopes that life may offer something better. One morning, another usual rainy day in the so-called summer holidays, I read in a woman's magazine of a short story competition for children.

'Why not have a go, Caroline?' I suggested. She was in the right age group.

She did have a go, writing about 'Micky, The Human Chimpanzee' – the problems of a monkey who thought he'd like to be a human, and decided to do something about it. He discovered, after various adventures – including falling in love with a girl human being, and finding himself invited to her home for tea – that it simply doesn't work trying to be someone, or something, that you aren't.

I'd suggested her writing the story to keep her occupied on another dreary morning, then thought that if we kept wasting stamps on competitions we were going to be even worse off than before. 'We'll buy a stamp and send it off, then we'd better not buy any more,' I said, looking inside my almost empty purse.

As it turns out, there are times when it does pay – speculating to accumulate, however depleted one's finances. It was fortunate that it had been a rainy day, and that Caroline had stayed in instead of going out to play, because a letter arrived some time later with the wonderful, astonishing news that Caroline had won first prize in the under-eleven section – £25 worth of premium bonds – not to mention the thrill of seeing her story, 'Micky, The Human Chimpanzee', published in *Woman's Mirror*. Perhaps for once it really had worked when we all whispered 'White Rabbit' on the first of the month! Best of all, we had been offered a much-needed injection of hope, that life would not always be so.

Most of us can get by skimping and scraping for a while. But few can exist without that very lifeblood of existence – hope. All of us should try and do something 'new' occasionally – something we never thought we could, or would even dare to attempt. Once the first timid steps are taken, and overcome, life can take on an entirely new and improved aspect – me with my Lollipop job for instance.

8

Excursions and alarms

From hardly knowing anyone in the neighbourhood when I stayed at home all day, wild cries of delight began to follow me wherever I went. Shopping in town during the summer holidays was a real eye-opener. When dressed up as best I could, trying to appear ladylike in high heels and dress, a voice would yell in high glee from somewhere: 'Mummy – look – look – it's the Lollipop Lady!'

My first instinct was to run. From the picture of myself standing at the crossing, in my barrage balloon coat, the pole with its huge hemisphere of scarlet and yellow in my hand, I felt out of place, a fraud, in my feminine dress and smart shoes. On the other hand, I may not be Prime Minister, or a famous actress, but I *had* a recognisable identity, if only that of a Lollipop Lady.

Then an arm enclosed my waist and a male voice interrupted my thoughts. 'Yes, it *is* our lovely Lollipop Lady! Fancy coming for a cuppa and perhaps an ice-cream for your daughters?' Yes please, we certainly did!

As we relaxed in the café, enjoying tea and cream cakes – luxury – the couple introduced themselves, and I recognised the little girl as Sandra, whom I took across the road daily.

'It's worth a bun and a cup of tea to know our Sandra's safe every day,' smiled Mrs Elton. 'Sandra thinks such a lot about you,' she continued.

That encounter was a highlight of the day. A few words of praise are worth any amount of money, and can help a person carry on when life is difficult. Mothers admire teachers, but I couldn't see them warming to the teachers enough to buy them tea and cream cakes. They tend to sense an intellectual barrier or something. With a Lollipop Lady it's different – I was one of them, like the window-cleaner or dinner lady. I'd worked in banks, offices, photographic studios and goodness knows where else, but, status apart, life on the crossing was the job I'd enjoyed best of all. The people I encountered had no pretensions. They were *real*, not putting on a superior act like those in up-market situations tend to do.

In mid-August we had a scorcher of a day – hot, with cloudless blue skies. Granville was having one of his week's holidays, an 'at home' one in the circumstances. He began by painting a sadly neglected drainpipe after finding an old tin of bright buttercup-yellow paint in the garden shed, so we didn't have to buy any.

'Hold the damned thing firmly,' he ordered, as I stood wavering at the base of the rickety old wooden ladder while he ascended. He had no head for heights, and neither had I, even when not on the first rung of the ladder. The prospect of him going up it was enough to create a nervous breakdown in both of us. So the bright sunflower yellow drainpipe continued to wear its ancient top half of rain-spattered grey after the paint brush was washed in turpentine and put away.

'Job completed,' announced Granville.

Another day he decided to straighten up the back garden, giving me some money saved from his pub job to take the children to York for a day out. There was a cheap day trip on a coach on Wednesday. Unfortunately my sense of direction is non-existent, unless it's in a straight line across my main road, and we lost our way back to the coach station after spending the afternoon in the Castle Museum. We hadn't enough money for any tea after paying the fare, so were just about all in, never mind the extra trailing about going up wrong turnings.

Everyone we asked was either 'Sorry, I'm a stranger here' or gave the wrong directions. I began to hate the sight of those city walls and tourist gift shops, and longed for old John the gardener, Brown Grandad, and all the familiar faces of my Lollipop days. We were due back at the bus station at six forty-five, but after comforting a small black puppy near the Shambles (which could be the name of my present life), and the puppy had narrowly missed being mown down by a car, Elizabeth decided she couldn't walk another inch without a Cola to drink. And Caroline needed to find a 'Ladies'. When we did find one it was crammed full of day-trippers with small children, including boys, small enough to squeeze through the steel barriers with the same penny. We were so short of money we did the same, making exhibitions of ourselves ducking beneath the turning steel arms.

By the time we came out the clock was already pointing to six thirty-five. Again we desperately asked directions, and were sent to a derelict wharf, someone else sent us back to where we'd come from, while a City Gent, quite out of touch with those who used public transport, shook his head sagaciously and twirled his umbrella in all directions, which only wasted more time. For once the heat was unwelcome. The August sun beat down ferociously as our nerves and tempers panicked. What would we do if the coach left us? I had no money for alternative transport.

Elizabeth began to shout and cry. 'I'll never trust myself to go anywhere with you again!' she sobbed. 'Why couldn't Daddy have come too? He wouldn't have got us lost.' And we might have had a car if it hadn't been for him, too, I silently fumed. Meanwhile Caroline saw the funny side of our predicament and ran here and there looking for the coach, sides aching with laughter.

So we lurched on, panting, pausing every few minutes to make breathless enquirings of leisured nit-wits. Then suddenly, like the longed-for Holy City, there it was, the bright red bus still waiting for us at five past seven, engines humming fretfully and faces, matching the redness of the bus, scowling ferociously out of the windows at us.

'D'you know what bloody time it is?' yelled one fat woman. 'Keeping everybody waiting like this, yer silly young sods.'

'Never again,' I said, as we sank into our seats. 'If this is holidaying on a shoestring I'd rather have no holiday at all.'

However, a pleasant, understanding old man who sat opposite us was sympathetic when told our story, and handed us a packet of mints.

'Take no notice of 'em,' he said. 'It happens to all of us at times.' And he winked.

'But to some more than others,' I managed to smile.

It was harder work than dashing down to the crossing and fitting in all the other jobs, pushing dolls' prams and their contents up and down our hilly West Riding roads the next day. Harder than working, desperately wondering how to pass the interminable weeks of the school holidays with barely enough to live on – yet preserving a semblance of 'having a good holiday'. At ten and twelve Caroline and Elizabeth reckoned they were too old to be seen pushing dolls in prams. Yet guilt overcame those sentiments when I pointed out that the dolls hadn't enjoyed a change of scenery for ages.

'We'll look like fools!' exploded Elizabeth.

'Oh come on,' said Caroline, 'they need a holiday same as anyone else.'

Cat-calls soon began to follow us up hill and down dale as our entourage progressed on the afternoon excursion.

'Oh, look! The Lollipop Lady pushing a doll's pram!'

I was relieved when the Annual Outing with the dolls was over, and they were safely stowed away again. But it had passed another day, perhaps taking the children's minds off the fact that we couldn't afford a proper holiday, going away to the seaside or somewhere.

'I bet the moneylender men have holidays,' scowled Elizabeth.

There were only two more weeks left before I returned to the Lollipop Beat. It couldn't come too soon. Although I'd hoped that some miracle would happen so we could take the children to the seaside, it hadn't. Each morning hope faded a little bit more, and initiatives of what to do next to pretend we were having a wonderful summer holiday diminished too. Tempers were fraying again.

Caroline, normally so pliable, refused to clear the breakfast dishes one morning while I cleared the ashes out of the grate. 'You're lazy,' accused Elizabeth. The long-awaited storm broke.

Caroline rushed upstairs crying uncontrollably, then re-appearing, red-eyed, with Elizabeth's school satchel packed for her departure, leaving home. Two pairs of navy knickers stuck out at the top, a summer dress, a pair of socks and a plastic mac – all her worldly goods.

How I loved them both, yet couldn't give them even a weekend holiday by the sea – and childhood, once gone, can never be retrieved. I wondered if those 'finance houses', who promise everything when victims go to them as a last resort, ever stopped to think of the effect their outrageously high interest rates had on their clients? My husband had gone to the first because he was too proud to borrow a then relatively small amount from his parents, or my brother, who was a bank manager, in his desperation not considering less expensive ways of borrowing money. A small advert in the local paper had started him on the road to near destruction, when he needed money in a hurry.

'But Caroline, please don't go – Prince will miss you, and so will all of us. Try and put up with us a little bit longer, it might all come right – eventually. Something is bound to turn up.'

Elizabeth gently took the satchel from her sister's shoulder. 'Don't go, Caroline – I'd have nobody to talk to and...' We were all crying.

Thus her disappearance into the Big Wide World, with only a couple of pairs of navy knickers and other bits and pieces, was averted.

Then we all burst out laughing when Elizabeth said, 'Besides, it's my satchel, and it's raining – you'd get soaked – and I didn't mean you were really lazy, Caroline. Shall we have a game of Monopoly?' So we did, all three of us.

Thank God for whoever invented Monopoly. Park Lane and all those posh places were ours for a brief time, and saved the day.

On another day of perpetual drizzle I suggested pretending to be Pickfords removals.

'Let's begin by moving the big wardrobe into the other bedroom for a change.' After all, a change is almost as good as a holiday. We always had fun moving the huge, given, old-fashioned pieces of furniture. It was a challenge, guiding the wardrobe without allowing it to become wedged across the banisters and making prisoners of the three of us for the rest of the day.

As we manoeuvred the big article out of the bedroom I soon doubted the wisdom of starting the task, but if it took our minds off the morning's post... Once begun, the rain and bills were completely forgotten. Every ounce of energy, enthusiasm and intellect was geared to manipulating the hulking object from one bedroom to the other. Had it been on casters it would have been far simpler. Granville, never much of a handyman, lived in Never Never Land – it was always 'One day we'll sell the damned lot, and get fitted wardrobes.'

Moving furniture suited Caroline's sense of fun down to the ground, so to speak. She shrieked with delight when very soon in the operation the wardrobe was wedged across the banister, and none of us could have escaped if the house had been on fire – roars of laughter when she saw my face anxiously peering round the stuck wardrobe, hugging herself with merriment at Elizabeth's pleas to be let out of the bedroom, the doorway having been blocked for the past half-hour.

'I want to go to the bathroom,' she wailed.

That was hilarious to Caroline.

When Granville returned it was to finish off the job of transferring the wardrobe, which we had somehow shifted so that the bathroom could be accessed, and we were all too exhausted to argue.

Because I was then earning a regular wage, even though only amounting to £3 14s 6d a week, I felt free to buy the occasional much-needed article for the house on the premise that, yes, there were outstanding bills – moneylenders taking the bulk of all we had – but if I hadn't been earning, what then? Besides, I was fed up to the teeth of apologising for old, broken-down chairs when anyone visited. Window-shopping in town, one of those long, tip-up seats caught my fancy. We were having coffee in one of the new, ultra-modern furniture stores that had strategically provided a coffee bar for customers, with a view of the irresistible furniture. One of those seats would add that touch of 'today' that our pre-war 'end of four' definitely lacked. It would fit beneath the dining-room window, and how it would save all that to-ing and fro-ing heaving armchairs out of one room to another when guests were coming.

A salesman with a little clipped moustache and eager eyes saw me hovering round the seat, peering beneath for the price ticket.

'Yes, madam, a bargain, isn't it? Only £16. Ideal when there are children. Keep the place tidy, somewhere to put their homework, your sewing books, magazines –'

I had a fleeting vision of the dining-room as we'd left it, with papers scattered over the floor, obliterating any carpet pattern. Mentally I tried to work out the number of weeks I'd have to man the crossing before it could be mine. Four, five…? I considered the advisability of putting all my money into the one item – there'd be nothing for weeks of my own then. Smiling, hopefully, the salesman waited.

I was determined to buy something new to brighten up the house, yet half wished that we'd never gone into the place. I wouldn't have seen it then. Impulsively I made up my mind.

'OK, yes. Put "Sold" on it, please. We'll have it on the three-month cash basis.'

As always, doubts assailed me as soon as the shop door closed behind us. Back home I felt myself going hot and cold, worried silly. What a fool – I'd landed us in even more debt. Much as I longed for some new furniture to brighten the drabness, I knew I shouldn't have done it.

Trembling, I dialled the shop number. 'Please will you cancel the seat I've just ordered – I've decided on something else instead. Mrs Wheeler.'

Oh, what a waste of time it had all been, all that looking, all that dithering. Then I tried to console myself that Prince would have wrecked it within a week. But I couldn't help feeling depressed. How pleasant it must be to be able to buy smart furniture, not to feel embarrassed when anyone called, hastily brushing cat hairs off decrepit old chairs, apologising all the time. Damn, *damn* the sodding moneylenders…!

9

Magic moments

*O*ne morning Elizabeth and Caroline thought it high time the dolls' hair was shampooed. The poor creatures were scooped up and carried outside, where they were unceremoniously flung on the back lawn to await their turn. Elizabeth had visions of being a hairdresser when she left school, and this was a practice run. Washing-up bowls, shampoo and cups for rinsing were arrayed on the grass. First, Walking Doll was stood in a bowl head first, long brown hair falling into the sudsy water. Rinsing the hair (the operation liked least of all by both children when it was their own hair) was performed with gusto and delight. If dolls could sigh with relief they must have done so as they were roughly towelled, then sat on an old pegged rug in the sunshine to dry.

We always had a six-monthly check-up with the dentist before school recommenced, and this time Elizabeth had to have two perfectly healthy teeth extracted. Though far from overburdened with money, both had too many teeth for the size of their mouths, so the dentist had to keep getting rid of the surplus to allow the others room to grow straight. It did seem a waste of good material.

On 26 August we went for a walk, taking a bag of carrots to give Tiny, the donkey at the Children's Home. We were in luck. Early blackberries were out, so we picked some and brought them triumphantly home to help out with a fresh fruit salad for tea. We never went for a walk in the countryside without taking bags or empty margarine containers, just in case.

Going for a walk, seeing beyond the Blue Horizon, all of us regained our sense of, well, it won't always be a rough ride. Beyond those fields, and woods, all manner of wonderful experiences could be there for us in the future. If only we could hang on…

The weather reverted to stormy and grey on the 29th. What to do now for entertainment? Elizabeth went to the supermarket and brought back, instead of the requested furniture polish in a tin, some spray-on stuff. It was the first time we'd had any, and the three of us went polish mad. We polished everything in sight – even Prince's fur didn't escape accidental attention – the Welsh dresser, dining-room chairs, and door. Then into the bedrooms, and the front room...

'Pooh!' gasped Granville, coming in from work at six, 'are you wearing some new perfume, or what?' Perhaps if we had polished more often it wouldn't have been such a shock.

Soon the end of the long, often rainy 'summer holidays' was in sight at last. On 30 August I called at the Education Office to be fitted for a new white mac for the warden job.

'You must have a short one, Hazel,' enthused the young man in charge. 'We like our girls to be "with it".'

I nearly added that on that lethal crossing, the chances were I'd soon be without it, whatever 'it' was.

It's all right being 'with it' in summer, or in warm weather, but in the autumn term warmth and sensible waterproofing was worth more to me than what I looked like.

But I had to accept the shortie, because there weren't any long ones left. It was made of linen, maybe cotton, for fine weather, while we wore the heavy plastic ones when it was wet. But how about those times when the weather could change from torrid heat one minute to a torrential thunderstorm the next? How did I decide which to wear? A Lollipop Lady can hardly taken an umbrella.

Quiet moments of relaxation are essential for mind, body and soul. That night, when Elizabeth and Caroline went to bed, there was a gorgeous yellow harvest moon. Granville was out working at the Fleece as usual, to keep our bodies and souls together. There was nobody to be romantic with, so I sat with Elizabeth and Caroline in turn, in their separate bedrooms, both at the front of the house, dreamily gazing out at that huge moon casting an unearthly spell over the landscape. Our house was directly opposite 'Oaklands', a very old stone house that for some years became a Home for Old Ladies. Trees spiralled their uppermost branches over the dark, weather-beaten rooftops. We felt as if we could have tirelessly watched the harvest moon indefinitely, as first it soared above a cloud, then a cloud drifted across it. We conjectured about the old, grey heads asleep on their pillows across the huge lawn opposite, and pondered how often they must have strolled with their lovers or husbands beneath other harvest moons in the early years of the century.

In other-worldly, quiet, reflective times such as those, the two children and I were entirely at one, all the frustrations of normal life far away. Until another day broke.

At the entrance to 'Oaklands', the old house, was a lodge, latterly unoccupied. In olden days, when a well-to-do family lived at the Big

House, a coach and horses used to take them to church on Sundays. A friend of ours used to live in the lodge, and she told us of peculiar happenings there. I related them to Elizabeth and Caroline as we knelt on a bed looking out on the moon-dappled lawn.

'Often, she heard the sound of horses, galloping, Mrs Richardson had told me, coming from the direction of the old stables. One Monday morning, getting on with the washing at the lodge, with never a thought in her head of ghosts, she suddenly heard the swishing sound of skirts going past. Looking up from the washing machine, she called, "Is that you, Susan?" Susan was her then schoolgirl daughter, and she's forgotten that she had already left for school, and shouted goodbye. Then she saw a child dressed in old-fashioned clothes – and realised it was a ghost.'

'But of who?' asked the children. 'Go on,' thoroughly enjoying the bedtime story that happened just across the road.

'Mrs Richardson went to see a lady who lived at the lodge before she did, and was told about a family with a lot of children who had lived at the lodge many years ago. In those days the bathroom had not been converted from a barn where the corn used to be kept. The children used to play there, and fashion corn dollies at harvest time. One of the children, a girl, developed tuberculosis, and died.'

Her description fitted exactly that of the long-haired child Mrs Richardson had seen while doing the washing that Monday morning.

No holiday is without its magic moments, and for us, watching that August harvest moon and listening to a true story of long ago, was one of them.

On the last day of August, a friend, also in the Authors' Circle of which I was a member, invited myself and the children to go with her somewhere for the day in her car. It wasn't often we had an outing by anything other than public transport, so we were delighted to have been asked.

'How about Bolling Hall, at Bradford?' she suggested. 'I'll bring sandwiches and a flask of coffee.' It goes without saying, that dismal summer, that as soon as we sat on a park bench for our picnic the heavens opened for the daily deluge.

'Run to the car, take cover,' yelled Miss Sayles, reminding me of wartime, with rain taking the place of the air raid siren.

If I'd had my Lollipop coat on, and knee-length wellington boots, I wouldn't have bothered. It can be refreshing out in the rain. However, the treat was a welcome change, and gratifying that someone was concerned about us enough to try and help us enjoy a small part of the holidays.

The weather didn't improve next day. But it was the first of September. School and September – don't they go together? So we chorused 'White

Rabbit' for luck and hoped for the best. We went to town, collected my retaining fee at the Education Office, did the shopping, then, rain inhibiting play outside, Elizabeth and Caroline amused themselves with jigsaws.

Time was creeping on, and still we hadn't managed to take them to the seaside. Then, like the cliff-edge moment of a film, when all seems lost, Granville announced that the landlord had lent him a few pounds, so he could take us all to Blackpool for the weekend. Now they would truthfully be able to say, when asked 'Where have you been for your holidays?', 'To Blackpool,' forgetting all those days of pushing dolls' prams and moving furniture to pass the time.

Even though it was only to be a weekend, school, and my reunion with Lollipop, would start again on the 7th. We'd made it! And Caroline's running away from home, over the hills and far away armed only with a school satchel and navy knickers sticking out of it, had mercifully been averted.

Saying 'White Rabbit' proved useless, though, as regards improving the weather. Four wet figures boarded a Yorkshire Traction bus for the Mecca of the North. I was secretly longing for it to be over, as nothing is so frustrating as trying to pretend you are enjoying squelching along a wet promenade, with expensive amusement arcades beckoning sodden holidaymakers inside. But Elizabeth was determined we weren't going to be shut away up some dark, dingy back street, as we were only going to be there for a weekend. So after making numerous enquiries, and everything too expensive, we finally discovered a small hotel just above the North Pier.

'Twenty-five shillings each for you and your wife, fourteen and six each for the girls,' said the landlady.

We had gone mainly for some sea air, so after dumping our luggage in the bedroom, found after seemingly miles of twisting, dark mahogany banisters, we strode out towards Bispham (there weren't as many slot machines and amusement arcades up there).

'Don't you wish we could afford a suite of rooms at the Imperial?' I asked Granville, holding his hand for once.

'I don't care where we are, as long as we are together,' he replied, and suddenly all the anger, resentment and disappointments of the summer, and the moneylending problems all disappeared like bubbles in the air.

We didn't find much exciting at Bispham – a few newsagents, a postcard shop selling saucy postcards, a few coffee bars, a mechanical horse where sixpence could be put in a slot to make it rock kiddies to and fro for a couple of minutes.

'Thank heaven for magazines,' I exploded, after buying a couple of girls' papers and a magazine and newspaper for ourselves.

'The sea's brown, not blue,' observed Caroline. It was, but the few stragglers bravely paddling in it looked blue enough.

Back for tea, to our dismay we had a table by the swing doors at the back of the dining-room, miles away from any sunshine that fitfully dappled the front tables. Gusts of wind blew in with late-comers or the waitress, or whoever kicked the door open. We shivered, and Granville turned up his coat collar after being the gentleman and swapping seats so he received the full onslaught of the draught.

'We can't complain – coming on spec, we're lucky to get in anywhere, at this price, too.'

'Beggars can't be choosers,' I couldn't resist replying.

10

'...noted for fresh air and fun'

When past the age of dancing and flirting in the Tower Ballroom or Winter Gardens on a Saturday evening, a traditional way of spending time and money is a trip to the Tower Circus. Not anticipating being in Blackpool, we hadn't booked in advance, and only gallery tickets were available. However, compared to what seats would have cost for four elsewhere, we readily snapped up the tickets.

How I wished we hadn't! As I've mentioned before, I don't like heights, not even the bottom rung of a ladder. I'd never been higher than the Circle before, and even then three or four rows back. To my horror we found ourselves on the first row, knees pushing through the bars that were the only thing separating us from the drop into space, then into the jaws of lions or whatever was performing. Elephants with long curling trunks were at the ready, poised to twirl any falling Lollipop Lady into the centre of the arena. Ferocious tigers pretended to be docile on their perches, but excited customers behind me were giving regular thrusts with their knees. Trying to force myself backwards was hopeless – looking down, with only a couple of bars between me and the fate below, was horrifying. It was like sitting on the edge of the world, waiting to be catapulted over the edge.

Waves of terror and faintness swept over me, a sensation I had never experienced on the crossing, despite horns blaring and traffic bearing down full tilt. How I longed to be able to exchange places with that, instead of the present nightmare.

'Are you all right?' I ventured to turn and look at Elizabeth and Caroline, though hardly daring to move lest I overbalance.

'I don't like sitting so high,' faintly replied Elizabeth. Caroline looked frozen to her seat, unable to speak or move. 'I daren't look down, Mummy,' she murmured.

Just before the lights dimmed and jazzy music introduced a prancing, jingling circle of dancing horses, I made a quick decision. Granville had nipped out to the Gents so wasn't there to consult. Not one of us could bear another second of that sensation of being in space, with nothing between us and disaster. But how to stand upright? What if nausea overcame us and we toppled over...?

'Follow me and don't look down,' I urged, feeling hot and dizzy, wanting to hold on to them but not daring to bend to hold their hands. 'Keep walking as though you are on an ordinary road,' I ordered, feeling far from being on an ordinary thoroughfare myself.

'Excuse us,' I muttered as people stood to let us pass. 'Please God, don't let them fall forward if their seats drop down,' I mentally prayed as we edged our way into the aisle.

'Thank God,' I said aloud as the three of us arrived safely at the end of the row, and climbed the stairs that put distance between us and that vertigo-inducing perch on the front row of the gallery.

Granville, returning from the Gents, thought he was seeing things as he encountered three tearful, agitated figures – the longed-for seaside holiday, and now this. Had we only ended up wasting more money?

The Manager was most understanding and, in the words of the Stanley Holloway monologue *The Lion and Albert* – also set in Blackpool – he agreed that 'no one was really to blame'. Granville managed to fumble in his pockets for a few extra shillings to enable us to sit in seats lower down that had been cancelled.

How fortunate that we don't all share the same phobias. Many wouldn't dare do my job as a Lollipop Lady for a pension, while I wouldn't dare be a cleaner-up in a theatre gallery, much less a trapeze artist or one of those incredible people who stand while somebody throws darts at them (well, as near as dammit) for all the money in the world.

Our troubles, when we returned to the cheap lodgings, weren't over by any means. The rain, which had fallen non-stop, was plopping all over the bay window and the surrounding bedroom floor, missing the bedclothes by inches. It was one of those so-called Family Rooms, so at least those who couldn't swim – all three of us – could have been rescued by Daddy, who could.

The owner and her husband were quite amiable when we complained. Privately I wondered if they imagined it to be an added feature for guests to wake up and find themselves practically adrift. They plonked a couple of thick travelling rugs on the floor to soak up some of the rainwater.

'I'll kill the bloody plumber if he doesn't attend to t'damned leak before winter sets in,' swore the husband.

Because the lodgings weren't one of those posh places where ample amusement could be enjoyed inside, Elizabeth and Caroline were determined that we went out, despite the absolutely torrential downpour and our lack of suitable clothing. Without a car, there's only a limited amount of outfits capable of being crammed into a case.

'Let's go and buy presents for Grandma and Grandad,' suggested Elizabeth. Lots of others had the same idea. Even before reaching the cover of the big departmental stores we were soaked. Raindrops trickled down our foreheads, noses, then chins, ending up trickling down the insides of our thin lightweight plastic raincoats.

We squelched round Lewis's and R. H. O. Hills until midday. Woolworths was so packed with pushing, disgruntled, jostling bodies that it was impossible to get inside.

As we splashed miserably up the steps of 'Belle Vista' the sun surprised us all by beaming out from a thick mass of grey cloud. Dammit, we then wished we were staying outside to dry off in its sudden glory.

We had fish and chips with 'doorsteps' of thickly buttered bread and strong tea, then draped macs, socks and shoes round the bedroom, hoping against hope that everything would be dry enough to wear in the evening.

After tea we queued with a mob of holidaymakers on the prom for a tram tour of the illuminations. We had to stand waiting for a long time, because although decorated trams were frequent, the main aim was to ride in the best one, which shone like a dragon in a fairy tale, so smothered in coloured electric lights. Open to the elements – the story of my life at the time – it was a colourful if cold ride. Back at 'Belle Vista' we had cream crackers, a nibble of cheese, and tea to drink, while exchanging holiday stories with other guests.

During any trip to Blackpool a visit to the Pleasure Beach is a must, although personally I could live without it. I hated being verbally bombarded by stall-holders. 'Throw a ball, madam?' 'Three darts for a tanner, sir? Win the missus a beautiful vase…' Who wants the junk, even if one wins? The pink and blue plush teddies that, unlike the stall-holders, had too little stuffing in them, chipped plaster rabbits, gaudy bracelets, and the sad trapped goldfish swimming endlessly round their globular prisons. All had the effect of making me feel depressed, exactly the opposite of what you're supposed to feel on a Pleasure Beach. Give me the natural, open countryside any time, where everything is free, and all the better for being so.

Far pleasanter was the saunter back, and conversation with an old age pensioner who was covered from the top of his balding head to the toes of his feet with squawking pigeons. He told us that he had been coming to a certain spot – by the North Pier – every morning for years to feed the birds. They knew him and he knew them, individually. He was worried about his friendship with the pigeons being curtailed, as the Council had begun frowning on those who fed them. What a pity, when both the old widower and the pigeons derived such pleasure from their morning meetings. I wondered how the Council members would like it if they were denied food?

There were just enough coppers left for Caroline to enjoy a few pony rides on the sands. Elizabeth wasn't keen on the idea of trusting herself to the idiosyncrasies of unknown ponies, so her share of what little was left went on a few slot machines, where she tried, unsuccessfully, to become a millionaire.

It was a blowy, non-too-promising afternoon, so we sat on hard wooden chairs to watch the outdoor performance of the Peter Webster Talent Show on the Central Pier. There were pink lettered sticks of rock, with 'Blackpool' imprinted on every bite, for the losers. 'Rock,' he said, disposing of the hopefuls, who most likely lost their teeth as well as their ambitions after numerous attempts at stardom.

Songs from *The Sound of Music* were belted out time after monotonous time, and we'd heard more than enough of 'Doe, a deer, a female deer' for one afternoon. Seaside 'Uncles' must have patience galore.

After the usual tea of ham salad, sliced bread and butter, tinned fruit cocktail and a dollop of ice-cream, followed by four 'fancies' on a doily-covered 'silver' cake-stand, with a few artificial flowers in the centre of a starched white tablecloth, Granville paid the landlady and we set off once more in non-stop rain for the homeward-bound Yorkshire Traction bus station.

How I longed for a car of our own! Humping wet cases on to the bus, often dropping them on other people's toes through sheer exhaustion, all hope of a brief period of summer seaside sunshine and happiness was finally shattered. Once settled in the bus, a baby screamed from journey's beginning almost to its end, while a couple of teenagers vied with the baby as to who could make the most noise as they blared continuous banal pop from a transistor.

The bus halted at a nondescript halfway dump for refreshments, which there was no time for after queuing with masses of other passengers outside the stinking 'conveniences'. How annoying to see men disappearing in and out of theirs in the twinkling of an eye. What a time-saver a trouser zip must be, and not having to sit down on something that so many others have already sat on – ugh! However, we needn't have panicked about the bus setting off without us. When we finally emerged, smothering ourselves with cheap Woolworth scent to disguise the horrible smells from that filthy wet hole, the bus refused to budge.

We took our places inside and sat like statues with the screaming baby and screaming transistor at full blast. If only the bus had started, and not them. After much grunting and groaning, the driver announced, 'There's nowt for it, ah'll have to telephone for a replacement bus,' then disappeared, leaving his passengers awaiting whatever fate had in store for them. To our dismay, a couple of fellows who looked like the village idiots turned up with a bag of tools. They fiddled around for some time, and whatever confidence I might have had about getting home the same day evaporated.

The lumbered up and down the bus steps. Then they attached a stout rope to the bus to try and yank it into action. The rope broke, snapped in two. Elizabeth, prone to hysteria, watched with an expression of abject terror, then dashed outside screaming.

'I'm not going up the Ainleys (a notoriously steep hill and accident black spot) on that bus! I'm not going up there – I'm staying here until a new bus comes!' At which pronouncement Caroline and I dashed outside to join the chorus of dissent.

'Get back inside while we have another go.' The two fellows threatened us with the end of the rope if we didn't obey.

I broke out in a cold sweat. Not having any scientific or mechanical leanings, I never have been able to understand how anything, weighed down with heavy bodies and luggage, could hoist itself, by stuff called petrol, up a steep hill without running backwards, even when in top-top condition.

'We'll stay in the Ladies all night rather than travel in a faulty bus,' I snarled. It only needs one to stand firm, others will soon follow. Had I not voiced disapproval the whole busload would probably have been towed on the end of that scraggy bit of rope. Even if it reached its destination, many might have been in a state of rigor mortis after the terror of ascending the Ainleys, one move forward and one terrifying jolt back.

Our longed-for holiday at the seaside was not over yet. Caroline, usually the calmest of the three of us, reacted once the new bus that turned up was on its way. With a driver hell-bent on making up for lost time, he drove so fast and furiously that we might just as well have been on the Big Dipper. Caroline's face was sea-green.

'Daddy, I feel sick!' The last straw – all over his new trousers that had cost a whole pound.

One of the passengers up at the front yelled to the Driver from Hell. 'Can you stop? A little girl's sick.'

The bus screeched to a stop as Caroline lurched down the aisle like a drunken sailor. With her Daddy they staggered down the bus steps, ending up in bending postures beneath the light from a street lamp.

Then the journey continued, intermittently halting for repeat performances along the highway, reminding me of the story of Hansel and Gretel, who dropped breadcrumbs so they would know the way back.

Our last buses had gone when we at long last arrived in town, so the driver drove us all to the garage to ask permission to take everyone home. Off we went, to outlying districts. I helped an ancient lady who had been due at her daughter's by ten o'clock; it was practically midnight, and she was terrified lest her daughter had gone to bed, all locked up, barred and shuttered for the night.

'What if I can't waken her up, what if I've to spend the night in t'porch – with her cat?'

I escorted her along the dark passageway to the back house where 'her Margie' lived. She wasn't the only one petrified with fear. I imagined hearing whisperings from every grating as we negotiated the narrow alleyway arm in arm.

'Ah didn't want a chap to come with me,' the old lady confided. 'That might have landed me in worse trouble than ever.'

I banged on the door. 'Our Margie', curling pins stuck out in all directions like road signs, shabby dressing gown pulled round her ample figure, came to the door.

'Nay, mother, where on earth 'ave yer been?'

'The bus broke down,' I explained, 'but all's well that ends well. Goodnight both of you. Pleasant dreams.'

I then ran back along the dingy passage to resume our seemingly never-ending journey with the disgruntled holidaymakers, anxious to get on their way.

It was well past two in the morning when we finally sank, exhausted, into our beds after the briefest 'summer holiday' of our lives. Worse, I longed to return to the comparative safety of the crossing. Imagine, more than six hours to get home to Yorkshire from Blackpool, a mere sixty miles or so, when scientists were putting all their energies into devising easier methods of reaching the moon. Where are the priorities?

The final day of the disastrous holidays of 1966 arrived. For Caroline it had been a complete wash-out. Still feeling sick, she stayed in bed until afternoon.

Annoyingly, as so often happens, glorious weather arrived when the holidays were over. A fresh breeze ruffled the trees, gold-tinted in their autumn splendour. The sky was duck-egg blue, the sun a picture-postcard gold. The enchantment coaxed Caroline from her bed. Groggily at first, she set out with Granville, Elizabeth and me looking for blackberries up the lane.

We all felt a bit like marathon runners, the finishing line in sight. We gathered sticks for the fire, too, to prepare for the chilly mornings ahead.

11

The electrician cometh

The seventh of September was a sunny morning, and it was strange having to get out of bed as soon as the shrill of the alarm clock sounded. Strange, not having time to make the beds, rake the ashes from the fireplace, or wash up before hurrying down to the crossing. Yet exhilarating to be out in the fresh morning air by twenty past eight.

I greeted Lollipop, down the snicket, like an old friend. Everyone agreed, although we had all needed a holiday, that it was good to be back – except the children. I enjoyed listening to what had been happening to regular users of the main road crossing over the past weeks.

Next day was just the kind of day we should have had at Blackpool, a day of warm sunshine, so warm that my hands could hardly bear to touch the stones of the old wall, they were so hot. Thursday was the same. That was wage day, but alas still only the holiday pay of thirty shillings. I never really got over the feeling that I'd worked a week for nothing when wages were retained a week in hand.

'I love September,' said John the gardener. 'Still summer, but things slowing down a bit. More time to stand and stare,' he grinned.

For me, the advantage was evenings that were light and warm enough to catch up on chores. There were no fires upstairs, and cleaning could be done in the evenings. It was still warm enough. And when homework was finished it was still light enough for Granville to take Elizabeth and Caroline to play putting in the park.

Nothing in this transitory life remains constant, however. By Monday the 12th I was standing at the crossing in wellington boots, white raincoat and upturned collar being pelted with torrential rain. It felt like I imagined monsoon rain to be like, violent. It was the same the next day. To add to the gloomy aspect I was due to have a check-up at the Health Department, one of those vile-sounding cancer smear tests. I often think that some of the things we have to put up with wouldn't be half as bad if they sounded better. 'Smear' conjured up such unpleasant visions…

'Ay, nowt to worry about, lass. You'll be all right,' was the general opinion when I mentioned where I had to go to some of my friends on the crossing.

I finished shopping in town, had the test (with eyes tight shut) and was home enjoying coffee and a cream bun by eleven. Then in complete contrast to the miniature heat wave of a few days earlier, I came home frozen stiff after the high winds and heavy rain of the midday and tea-time stints at the crossing. But variety is what I enjoy. At least I wasn't trapped in the high-up gallery at Blackpool Circus!

It was a wonderful feeling when the allotted days passed by and there was no letter asking me to go again to the Health Department. We may have had moneylenders breathing down our necks, but at least I was fit, and could fight them off eventually. I have never smoked a cigarette in my life, and am sure fresh air and exercise help greatly in keeping fit. All the more reason for being on the 'Lollipop Beat'. Despite all the bad weather, I never had a cough or even a sniffle, while many office workers were regularly off work. Even so, fresh air fiend though I was, I was so chilled through that I was glad to stay in by the fire most evenings, reading or knitting with Prince snuggled up on my knee.

Next morning the plumber arrived early to put a new copper pipe wherever it is that pipes are put in a kitchen. I detest having workmen in the house.

'Lovely morning,' was my opening gambit to the doleful little putty-faced man in squashy flat cap.

'Aye,' came the noncommittal reply.

I never know whether to watch the proceedings, or shut myself away – but do that and he'll think money is no object, and he can go as slowly as he wants. I baked two dozen buns once, in the hope that a visiting electrician would enjoy a couple and establish a bond of friendship between us. In an effort to be matey I joined him for coffee, only to be reminded of a children's serial I once saw, *The Clutching Hand*.

'Ee, they're right tasty, these,' the electrician decided, grimy paws shooting out for another, then another, until the first dozen were devoured. I vowed never again to put so many buns in front of a workman... And what a mess the bedrooms were in after he left. One was still uncarpeted – we had left it until the extra light sockets had been fitted. But did the electrician dump his filthy tool bag on the bare floor? Oh no. He had dragged it along the front bedroom carpet, the newly fitted pampas green one. Huge black fingerprints punctuated the white banisters, and to crown it all, when Granville returned from work, he was livid with rage.

'What the bloody hell do they think they're doing?' he asked, more or less implying it was my fault, and I ought to have known. They had put old-fashioned switches on the skirting boards, and instead of lying flat against the wall, they protruded three or four inches into the room. So instead of being of being free from workmen, I had to encounter the fools next day and go through the whole performance again. The second batch of buns was scoffed. I don't like to appear to be a Mrs Scrooge, but it meant baking again when I came in from the crossing.

Caroline, examining her rocking-horse, which, three years earlier, at Christmas 1963, had cost fifteen guineas, cried, 'Those men have been riding on Lilac Domino, and left dirty fingermarks all over her!' I was furious – hard up, then paying for time spent in such a way. Firms should instruct their employees how to conduct themselves in other people's homes! Maybe apprentices take advantage of the fact that so many women go out to work, and they feel at liberty to do as they please. Granville telephoned the firm and complained, and the boss came to inspect the blackened carpet where tools had been thrown down and a dusty black bag dragged across, as well as the wrong switches, the fingermarks and the damaged rocking horse.

I was not a coward on the crossing, but as nine thirty drew near, and my return home was imminent, to where those workmen were, my brain flashed around for escape routes. The boss had been given our door key, so the culprits could let themselves in. How would I greet people we had complained about the day before? 'Hello, don't get up to any tricks today, will you boys?' or 'Now then (in stentorian voice), I hope there won't be a repetition of yesterday…' I may have some authority on the crossing, but in my own home, faced with such uncouth louts, I felt I had none at all. So I dawdled to the shops, hoping for once that many had to be served before me. Then, while slowly wending my way up the aisle in the supermarket, a voice hailed me (I'm easy to see among other shoppers in my white Lollipop coat). It was Dorothy, a friend who was also in the Authors' Circle. Usually I was in too much of a hurry to talk, but today, 'Talk with me a while, Dorothy,' I implored. 'I can't bear the thought of being in the house with those men again.'

'Come down to our house for coffee then,' she suggested, always ready with a helping hand.

It did seem silly, trailing heavy shopping through the short cut in the wood, rather than taking it straight back home, then having to drag two heavy baskets all the way back again. Fancy, a mature adult not daring to enter her own house! Had it been the children shying away from such a situation I'd probably have given them a sermon on Facing Up To Life. Oh yes, it's far easier to give advice than to follow it! After wasting an hour at Dorothy's, thinking how many jobs I could have done had I gone straight back home, I had to return whether they were there or not. Time was flying and I had to get the shopping in the house somehow before the next crossing session at twelve. On tip-toe I stealthily approached the front door, quaking as though I was breaking and entering someone else's property. I made a mad dash through the hallway to the kitchen and plonked the baskets on top of the washing machine before slamming out of the front door again, meaning to go up the lane to a neighbour's, Mrs Broadbent, and ask if I could stay there till nearly crossing time. But my plan was thwarted. No sooner was I half running, half walking towards the row of cottages where she lived, than a rough voice bawled after me through an open bedroom window.

'Hoi, there – Mrs Wheeler – will you be in after dinner? We're not finished yet.'

My heart sank – not finished, and the boss had promised I wouldn't be inconvenienced for more than an hour or so. All cowardice vanished beneath a rising tide of anger. Now we were face to face, I let fly, telling them exactly what I thought. 'Go!' I commanded, caring not a damn who or what was passing. 'Get out of the house and never come back.'

Imagine, a couple of little whippersnappers like those had had me scurrying about like a scared rabbit. The cheekier of the two yelled, 'Aw, stop making a scene and get back to yer Lollipop!'

Fuming, I raced back into the house and stampeded upstairs to see what damage they had done this time. One bedroom door had been pulled off and was hanging, swaying precariously on its hinges. Trembling, this time with rage, I picked up the telephone and demanded to speak with the boss, immediately. I told him about the latest misdemeanours.

'I'm terribly sorry, Mrs Wheeler, I'll send someone else at once.' He apologised profusely, and the next chap turned out to be all right.

A couple of days later all was forgotten in the sudden burst of golden sunshine after early mist. As the day progressed it became hotter and hotter, and all the girls came out in summer dresses again. And for the afternoon session I wore the white cotton coat instead of the heavy plastic mac, and sandals. My feet were so comfortable I felt I could literally float along with the 'STOP – CHILDREN' pole.

Idylls don't last, though. I suppose in a way that's why when we are happy we only realise we are because of the contrasting drabness and unhappiness of unhappy times. There's no yardstick to measure even ecstasy against if every moment is ecstasy. Or if we had champagne every day, how we'd long for a draught of water from a brook. On 22 September, back swung the weather to the darker side. The morning crossing was misty and cold, with not a semblance of sun all day long. The next day continued grey too, an exhausting, monotonous grey, such an exhausting greyness that after midday crossing I allowed myself to have a nap – quite an event for me.

Contrast is better. The 25th was foggy at first, car headlights dazzling me from the gloom, children's mouths muffled with woolly scarves, giggling at the first intimation of good things to come in the autumn term – like pea-soup fogs, and even, perhaps, snow. What fun they'd have snowballing the Lollipop Lady!

Anything that slows down my usual quick walking pace I loathe. So one day, after riving hard skin from my foot (couldn't afford to go to a chiropodist), possibly having formed with all the pounding backwards and forwards on the crossing, I woke to find I could hardly bear to put my foot on the ground.

'What's matter wi' thee, lass?' asked John the gardener, as I hobbled painfully across the road. 'Atta trying out a new one-step dance or what?' That morning, had a car come down the main road at top speed, expecting me to nip smartly out of the way, they'd have had a dead body on their hands – complete with self-maimed feet.

The last day of the month was more of a rush than any other. Granville's salary was in the bank, so after morning crossing I always rushed into town on the first bus after I'd garaged Lollipop down the snicket, with the bottom of my basket inches deep in bills to be paid. I would queue in the bank to withdraw his wages, then queue to get rid of them at the coal merchants, electricity, gas, television rental, the monthly payment to the court (so humiliating), and various other places. I was on my feet from seven till eleven thirty non-stop. Then, receipts safely stowed away under packets of bacon, cheese and other commodities, I would treat myself to a cream cake from the confectioner's. Small treats can make all the difference between wanting to live or to give up.

On a bus homeward-bound at last, I dreamed of ten minutes with feet up, a teacake sandwich, coffee – gallons of it – and the once-a-week indulgence of a chocolate éclair or cream-filled meringue and a quick flip through a magazine. Heaven!

The only drawback marring my brief escape from work was the fact that the radio had to be on for a time check, or I could use the mill buzzer, which hooted at midday. If I shot out of the door like a bullet from a gun as soon as the buzzer began, emulating an Olympic runner, I was able to arrive, panting, at the crossing and grab Lollipop from across the road down the snicket. Those children going home for midday meals appeared just about a few minutes later. If a police car streaked past I tried to appear cool, calm and collected, not still halfway in a dream over a romantic short story I'd been reading and left open on the dining-room table. I was sure that the police checked up on whether or not I was there on time. However, I'd got the timing to a fine art, always there for the first comer from school.

My foot still wasn't healed, so I made an appointment with a chiropodist. Twelve shillings and sixpence out of my wage didn't leave much over that week, which was especially aggravating as I'd been hoping to save enough for an autumn suit to wear on our Wedding Anniversary on 2 October. On that day, as usual, nothing went right.

'Happy Anniversary!' Granville wished me. Permanently short of cash, he handed me a tiny, cheap bottle of scent. Phul-Nana – a thumbnail full of trash. Before his dumbfounded gaze, I poured it down the sink – a complete waste of one and eightpence. It was Sunday, and we had been married for fourteen years. It was a brilliant day weatherwise, but emotionally awful.

'I might as well go and see my mother then, if that's your attitude,' my husband of fourteen years sadly announced. We all ate breakfast in an aroma of Arabian Nights-like Phul-Nana.

'It's not that I want expensive gifts,' I sobbed. 'But I bet wives of those moneylenders get eternity rings and taken out for a meal on *their* wedding anniversaries, paid for by you, and others they have in their web too. Bloody parasites that they are – we'll never escape their clutches.'

Elizabeth, sensing a Day of Discord, pushed her plate of cornflakes away. 'I'm going. I'm going to my Grandma's.'

The door slammed after Granville's departure. Then after Elizabeth. Caroline I were left with the Celebration Chicken (smallest in the shop) cooking in the oven and nobody to eat it but us. So when it was ready, I put it in an empty shoe box, which was a perfect fit – size 5 – and off we went to mother's as well. What a wedding anniversary!

Still sulking, I slept with Elizabeth that night and pondered anniversaries. Why did some wives receive bouquets of flowers, magnificent cards declaring everlasting love and devotion, plus a candlelit romantic dinner with their husband, while mine always fell flat? I knew the answer: because a rash decision to borrow money had led us into a fix that neither of us had any idea how to get out of.

12

Chapter of accidents

'What a foul, consistently rainy day,' I wrote in my diary for 3 October. 'Soaked on crossing every time. In between soakings nothing but boring jobs. Making beds, tidying up, washing up.'

After tea the telephone rang.

'Hello, Mrs Wheeler. Matron here, from "Oaklands" (the Old People's Home across the road). I wonder if your Elizabeth or Caroline can help with my violin if I pop over, please?'

''Course they can,' I answered for them.

Matron had begun learning the instrument again after years of non-practice. 'I thought it might be a soothing relaxation after dealing with the old ladies,' she explained. We punctuated the impromptu lesson with lots of hot coffee and my home-made ginger biscuits.

On 4 October I began wearing trousers for work, besides wellingtons and the heavy raincoat.

'Here you are, luv,' a sympathiser said, handing me two pairs of heavy navy trousers she had grown too fat for. 'These should keep you a bit warmer this cold weather.'

'Thank you ever so much.' I was so grateful, having to change trousers sometimes after becoming almost drenched every duty. Walking home I nearly sank under their weight over my arm. They seemed to weigh almost a ton, and were probably manufactured about the year dot, when weight was the answer to winter chills. They turned out to be extremely warm, and when one pair was splashed heavily I hung them over the creel to dry and wore the other pair.

Those October days the rain plop-plopped as though it might go on for ever. Brown and gold leaves underfoot were saturated, and depressing compared to when they had been glinting in the sunshine. Sometimes in quiet moments I looked up into those leaden skies and conjectured what the world would do if God forgot to turn the tap off in them...

74

But there was always Thursday, pay day, to look forward to, and the excitement of looking through the letter pages in magazines in W. H. Smith, to see if I had won a guinea for a letter, and passing the quiet moments when nobody was about wondering how best to spend my £3 14s 6d wage. On Thursday I usually went on the nine thirty-five trolleybus into town, cursing if a latecomer ran down and forced me to miss it – I daren't risk a child crossing alone, even if it was his or her fault for being late. I signed for my wages, transferring the contents from buff-coloured envelope to purse. Hooray! Ready for a spending spree! I loved to surprise the family on Thursdays, either with something new for them to wear, or a special treat for tea.

That week is was new cardigans for the children. One cost 21s 11d for Caroline, while a larger navy one for Elizabeth cost 29s 11d. Then I saw some cosy-looking pastel-shade flannelette sheets, only 14s 11d each, so bought one in yellow. It was strange, but however heavy the load was after shopping, the happier I felt, having been able to buy something to please those I loved so very much. Yes, when I was a Lollipop Lady Thursdays were happy for me – a bit like having Christmas Day every week. Fridays were happy, too, filled with thoughts of what to do on Saturday and Sunday, two whole days to myself, not chopped into portions. I might even start writing a book. A stay-at-home housewife tends to forget how exciting Friday, the end of the working week, can be, anticipating leisure after the pressures of keeping to a timetable. It was almost worthwhile going out to work just for the sensations of pay days and Fridays alone.

One Friday morning a young mother was in too much of a hurry to get to the end of the week. There was a slight fog over the crossing, and the trolleybuses were 'running on teacakes', as the saying went in our part of Yorkshire when things were going awry. She and her small daughter Debbie rounded the corner to the bus stop. I was already in the centre of the crossing with a group of children, awaiting an opportunity to cross the rest of the way. A bus loomed up behind us, out of the gloom.

'Go on Debbie,' shouted her mum, glad she wouldn't have to wait for another bus. 'Run across to Hazel.'

Debbie swooped across before I had time to swing round and yell, 'No – wait!' I also had to watch that none of my youngsters in the middle of the road decided to dash the rest of the way on their own without my saying it was safe. There was a sickening sound of brakes, and my stomach churned over as I glanced round to see what had happened.

Debbie was shaken and in tears, after running back on to the pavement. A car, swerving out from behind the bus, had continued on its way. Her mother had to miss the bus after all. She was nearly the cause of her daughter being in an accident that no one, not even me in charge of the other children, could have prevented.

I felt wild with anger when parents took the law into their own hands. Had something happened, the Lollipop Lady or Man would obviously be the one accused of negligence.

'I'm so sorry,' Debbie's mother apologised when I crossed back to their side of the pavement. 'I was stupid telling her to dash across to you. All for the sake of saving five minutes catching the earlier bus.'

But Debbie was so upset that she held on to her mother's hand, refusing to let go, and her mother lost more time having to take her all the way to school.

After heavy rain cleared the mist, the rest of that day was an absolute treat to be outside – a gloriously golden, picture-calendar type of day. Blue sky, fleecy clouds, leaves crisply gold, brown and russet, crackling underfoot. A Good-To-Be-Alive Day, with leaves blowing in the occasional breeze like miniature Margot Fonteyns and Pavlovas, pirouetting gracefully down to earth.

Wanting to remain outside as long as possible, feeling healthy and happy as a young animal, I decided to go into town after the nine thirty finish. I tucked Lollipop away down the snicket, lifted my shopping basket from the wall and caught a bus. Lots of non-working women were resplendent in the morning sunshine in smart tweedy suits and court shoes, off to sip morning coffees in leisurely fashion in one of the smart cafés – Field's, Sylvio's, or Whiteley's – and meeting friends to gossip.

Dressed as I was, in fisherman-like, mud-splattered, stub-toed wellingtons, conspicuous white Lollipop mac and navy beret, usually I went home for my coffee. But as I whizzed round the shops that morning, I bumped into an old friend, dressed up to the nines, even to painted fingernails.

'Oh Hazel! Come for coffee, I'm dying to have a chat with you.' Hazy blue smoke rings spiralling from her cigarette, held in fingers adorned with rings.

'But look at me – how I'm dressed. More for a fish-market,' I demurred, taking in her svelte brown velvet suit and matching high-heeled shoes. 'What if somebody else sees me in this pantomime get-up – or an ex-boyfriend? No, I prefer to dash home, out of sight.'

Undeterred, Pat grabbed my arm, steering me into the market. 'There'll be nobody here to worry about. The coffee's good and strong, and we can talk.'

Dress does not, or should not, make the man – or woman – I know. But I do think it makes them decide what kind of establishment they may grace with their presence. I'd rather have *died* than enter one of those posh cafés dressed in Lollipop garb.

So there we sat, among the down and outs, at nine forty-five – too early to be among the toffs for morning coffee, while grubby little waitresses with fag ends drooping out of the corners of their mouths wiped over Formica-topped tables and dropped ash on to the floor.

Everybody seemed to be on first-name terms with everybody else. 'All right, Harry?' 'The usual, Elsie?' I wished I could have drunk the coffee without my lips having to come in contact with the chipped, brown stained cup. Discreetly, I turned it round, so I wouldn't be drinking from the side everybody else did.

'See that old guy?' Pat said, pointing to an old fellow at the next table, scraggy necked, striped muffler loosely tucked into the neck of a check, tatty shirt. 'He's ninety-three. Comes in every day for a bowl of soup.' (I wondered how Pat knew – as she aspired to more aristocratic circles.)

He scribbled something on a scrap of paper, the bowl of steaming tomato soup cooling by his elbow. He beckoned to the waitress. ''Ere, miss, will she take this cheque, think yer?'

The dumpy manageress smiled good-naturedly.

'It's all right, Dad – have this one on us. Nice to see you again.'

Our waitress told us that same performance was enacted daily.

'I can't see such generosity and humanity displayed in those posh places,' I remarked to Pat.

She smiled. 'That's why I come here. They're real people.'

Next morning was autumn perfection once again. To add to its delight, mother turned up in working mood. She cleaned the kitchen, including turning out a couple of cupboards that had been awaiting my attention for, well, maybe a year or more.

Thursday brought heavy rain, but it was pay day, so tolerable. Friday 14 October on the crossing was a hazy, golden, beautiful morn. In between rushes of children and exchanges of 'Good morning' with those rushing for their usual buses, I kept looking up and marvelling at that wonderful blue-pink early morning sky. It reminded me of one of those old-fashioned watercolour paintings. What lie-abeds miss when they don't get up to see such beauty! How can anyone be bored, or feel that life cannot alter for the better, when there are skies such as those to gaze up at?

Yet many are so busy they never have time to stand and stare. As a Lollipop Lady I had, and was glad. Everyone faces difficulties, some tragedy, but if only we remember to look up, there is hope. The loveliness of the seasons never dies.

At tea-time Brown Grandad shambled up to show off Beverley's gaudily crayoned pipe container, made from a big cornflake packet. Across the side was printed 'PIPES.'

'Damned good, don't you think, Hazel?' proudly smiled Brown Grandad, before scurrying after the artist.

That evening, with the 'Lollipop Beat', as I sometimes called it, over for another weekend, we all went to a coffee evening at the newly opened YMCA in town, arranged to promote friendship between overseas students and local residents. It was most enjoyable, listening to lifestyles different from our own.

Next week began on Monday with an accident. It was sunny and warm, exactly the right conditions for gossiping. The warmth of the sun penetrated to my back, making me feel energetic and glad to be there. The Junior School secretary and I were enjoying our usual twenty-minutes-to-nine chat, complimenting the weather man. We turned quickly, hearing the strident sound of a motor bike screeching in our direction along the main road.

In a split second, both of us knew something terrible and unavoidable was about to happen. There was a much slower moving lorry immediately in front of the motor bike, and the lad on it was travelling much too fast to pull up in time. There was nothing either of us could do but stand and watch in horror as the bike hurtled head on, crashing into the back of the lorry. It was like watching an Alfred Hitchcock thriller, seeing the danger but totally incapable of averting it.

We stood transfixed after the impact and bang, as the youth was flung into the air like an inconsequential rag doll. Back on terra firma, the heavy motor bike somersaulted a few inches away from us, coming to rest across the now unconscious boy. Children gathered round me, saucer-eyed at the scene in front of them. They were reluctant to go across the road with me, wanting to remain until the ambulance arrived.

'Is he dead?' they asked. Only then did the momentarily stunned secretary dash across to the telephone box. Fortunately it was in working order.

Then Reg, a neighbour, who worked at the ambulance station, happened to come round the corner in his car on his way to work. Out he sprang and rushed over to the casualty, whose legs and feet were beginning to move stiffly up and down beneath the bike. Then a few more men arrived on the scene, carefully easing the machine off and moving the lad to the side of the road.

An ambulance and police car screamed up. It would just be at the busiest time, when lots of traffic was flying past, taking owners to work. The motor bike was propped against the wall where I stood, and stayed there for the rest of the day, a great source of wonder and excitement to the schoolboys who went up to it, touching it in awe and reverence. It obviously did not deter them in the least from coveting such a bike themselves.

The youth lived, after suffering concussion and broken legs. He was lucky to have been wearing a crash helmet. It had started out such a beautiful morning. What a shame to miss it in a haze of oblivion.

Everything soon returned to normality, with the usual small incidents and small talk. An elderly Grandma explained to me how she conserved her energy.

'I haven't enough energy to use twice over,' she sighed, clutching the hand of her bright-eyed granddaughter. 'So if I'm going out in the afternoon I refuse to romp with Sarah in the morning – little devil that she is.'

Sarah stuck out a disapproving tongue.

'So I'm staying in this afternoon listening to *Woman's Hour*, with me knitting and me feet up,' Grandma whispered confidentially, ending with a hoarse giggle, as if she was doing something wildly exciting.

After politely giggling with her, and taking them to the other side, I was hailed by the local piano teacher, who was sixty-ish and lived alone in a confusion of music scores.

'Come along now, Hazel, get on with your job,' she ordered, with an imperious flourish of a letter. 'You know I hate crossing this road, so you'll post this for me, won't you?'

The letter box was only at the end of our lane, so I did it there and then, secretly wondering, 'Am I supposed to be an odd job man for them all?'

'I'll look after t'crossing,' she grinned, but I was back in a couple of seconds. She was hoping for a chat.

'I've knitted dozens of pairs of slippers in thick rug wool, all in different sizes,' she told me. 'They're all lined up in the hallway, so my pupils can change into some as soon as they come for their lesson. Or in bad weather my carpets would be in a worse mess than this 'ere road,' she chuckled. Miss Taylor wore what looked like a tea-cosy, knitted in bright red thick rug wool, pulled low over her eyebrows and hiding her ears. She was a good customer at the little wool shop down the road.

If only I dare put slippers for my guests to change into! But I daren't. If only taking shoes off in rainy weather was taken for granted, and not regarded as the hostess being 'Old Maidish' – and why aren't workmen told to change out of filthy boots before entering a house they are to work in? And, oh, if only we dared stop unthinking guests draping wet outdoor coats on beds!

Miss Taylor soon enlisted Elizabeth and Caroline as piano pupils. They told me that she always greeted them at the door beating time to music with a stick.

While some of my 'customers' changed their outfits daily, some, like Miss Taylor, saw no point in it when clothes weren't dirty. So, like me in my white Lollipop coat, she was identifiable by her red woolly cap. It never occurred to her not to wear it, even in summer weather, nor to be at all concerned never to have married. She was, I supposed, 'married' to her music.

And, unlike so many ordinary marriages, happy with it.

13

Counting blessings

Timmy, a tiny striped tabby who had recently come to live up the lane, at the lower end by the crossing, proved to be delightful – but a bit of a problem. He took an enormous fancy me and Lollipop, and a favourite pastime was scrambling up it when I wasn't aware he was there. It was awkward when I'd set off with a crowd of schoolchildren into the middle of the road to hear them squeal, 'Mrs Wheeler – you've got a cat up yer Lollipop!'

The only thing I could do was continue, as all the traffic had come to a halt for me to see the children across. Some of the motorists honked their horns in amusement at the sight of a Lollipop Lady escorting a tabby kitten across clutching the pole. I dreaded Timmy leaping down and shooting off beneath the cars – mercifully he clung on grimly until we reached the pavement once more.

A few times I carried him home, pushing him through the garden fence then dashing back, warning the children to stay where they were until I returned. Mrs Byford promised faithfully to keep him inside the back garden. But how can a cat be restrained? It can leap over walls and fences in search of more adventure in the Outside World. So, a few minutes after the promise I'd see Timmy again, his little striped face full of curiosity about my antics, while Mrs Byford, acutely embarrassed in hair curlers and headscarf, stood at her front door shaking a duster, and her head.

I also felt extremely concerned about a wiry fox terrier. The colour of a russet autumn leaf, he spent all his days briskly trotting up and down the road, along the pavement, back by the park, then down the lane to the crossing again. I half expected him to take out a watch from a waistcoat pocket, like the Rabbit in *Alice in Wonderland*, and mutter, 'I'm late – I'm late – for a very important date…', keeping up the same brisk pace to make onlookers, and me, think he was about Important Business, brown eyes looking straight ahead, neither to right nor left. I'm sure he'd have felt so ashamed had he realised that we knew he had nowhere to go – that his owners left him out all day while they went to work.

The poor little creature was trying to appear so businesslike, when in reality he was desperately simply passing the long hours from eight in a morning till half past five, tea-time, when the young couple who owned him returned from work. How those hours must have dragged on cold, wet and miserable days, then in the snow of winter. I tried to imagine what ports of call he might find – seat beneath a shelter in the local park? Huddled beneath a house porch? How I hated owners such as he was unfortunate enough to have. It was as despicable as keeping a dog shut up indoors all day long. Do they give a thought how an intelligent animal passes the time? It can't sleep *all* the time, after sleeping during the night. It can't read, switch on the radio, or even do the housework. I bet they would if they could. If boredom drives incarcerated animals to distraction, and he chews slippers and other articles, he's a 'bad boy' and chastised. Truly, a dog's life for many.

But I was as glad for Sandy, as I learned he was called, when we had a day of warm sunshine, as I was for myself, especially if the good weather lasted through all his numerous circular tours.

Brown Grandad emerged, puffing and blowing, from his first morning duty as I helped other children across the road. Retirement must be a glowing time of life for some, if active and in good health, and at liberty to face each new dawn with no guilty feelings about passing the day exactly as one pleases. Only at the onset of life is a person as free, in early childhood, before school and then work pinions mind and body into set routines.

Brown Grandad had a kind little wife at home to dust and cook for him, a little, mousy-haired, docile woman who obviously adored her husband of many years. That day being a perfect autumnal one, he had told her she needn't bother about lunch. They'd have something cooked for tea.

When he appeared to collect Beverley at the last crossing of the day he was beaming with happiness.

'Where have you been today?' I asked as he paused to chat after his constitutional.

'Oh, it's been glorious!' he enthused. 'Wonderful! Over the hills, over the moors, heavenly.' He handed me a bunch of bright purple heather. 'Shove that in a vase, Lollipop.'

Brown Grandad looked glorious too, I thought, with clean white hair, slicked back from twinkling eyes, the tan of outdoor days still clinging to his kindly face. He twanged his braces as he waited for Beverley.

'First I went by bus to Almondbury – cuts out climbing that steep hill – then I sauntered round by Farnley Tyas, and called for a pint and ham sandwich at t'Farnley Cock. Had a bit of a natter with a couple of blokes – ah yes, it's been glorious. Simply glorious!'

Then Beverley appeared, peeping out from the snicket to see if Grandad was there to meet her. I went over, back to the other side, then waved goodbye as they walked happily home.

Brown Grandad told me that his daughter was expecting another baby soon, so it looked as though he'd have a job for a long time to come yet. Not world-shattering news, but lives of ordinary, good people like Brown Grandad meant more to me than what happened to Elizabeth Taylor or Richard Burton. I hoped he would be presented with a grandson next time.

'I'm set on having a little lad to take to rugger matches with me,' he confided. 'On Saturday afternoons.'

The next child to appear from the snicket was Mark, the milkman's little boy.

'When is half term, Mark?' I asked conversationally.

'Oooh,' he breathed, eyes wide as milk bottle tops. 'When t'witches come out!'

Matron from the Old People's Home hurried round the corner, beaming at me.

'Mr Shaw was so pleased with me last night. He's given me my first piece to practise on me violin.'

How I enjoyed being told about all the small triumphs that made up people's lives.

Back home from the crossing, I wasn't pleased with Prince. She gave me a vindictive nip at the back of my ankle because I dared to make coffee before giving her milk and pilchards.

Next morning the Head of the Junior School stopped his car at eight forty-five. Looking first left, then right, then left again, he came over to where I stood.

'Oh, what have I done?' was my immediate reaction. When someone in authority approaches me I always think I'm in the soup for something or other. Heart thudding madly, I tried to look as intellectual as possible, hiding Lollipop behind my back.

'Ah, Mrs Wheeler....' Hands thrust deep into the pockets of his smart sheepskin car coat, he peered at me over bifocals. I didn't like being scrutinised through those. 'I'd just like to know, at first hand, how our children are behaving on the road.'

The previous afternoon a couple of policemen had visited the school to give a talk on road safety, and to show a film on the subject. Road accidents are tragic. But there are other tragedies I hear about on my crossing. I assured the headmaster that the children are well-behaved and responsible, on the whole. He gave a kind of salute, then went back to his car.

A lady rushed up to me, wanting my attention before anyone else took precedence.

'Have you heard?' she panted. I heard a lot of things. 'About young Mrs Parnaby?' my informant continued. For some months I had exchanged a few words with the young woman as she went for the bus, for her appointment at the Maternity Home for pre-natal check-ups.

'No, how is she? She was so excited about having a baby. All the matinée coats she was knitting...'

The person before me nodded her head, sadly. 'Changing the name they were going to call it every other day – couldn't wait for the Big Day.'

'We saw it in the paper – she had a baby girl, didn't she? Fiona Mary, I think they were calling it. I said to Granville, Mrs Parnaby will make an ideal mother – she'll have a stocking full of soft toys and rattles for Christmas already.'

The tragic expression deepened.

'Oh yes, she had the poor little thing. But it died, of gastroenteritis while still in the Maternity Home. Fancy, after only four days of life...'

What on earth could I say when next I saw young Mrs Parnaby? She would now be thin, and full of sorrow, not of plans for her baby's future. I couldn't imagine the pain of it.

'But perhaps there will be other years, and other babies – yet the first born, even if only lent for a little while...'

'Yes, I know, always holds an evergreen corner in a mother's heart,' sighed my acquaintance, as she put her hand out to get on the trolleybus.

Another familiar figure rounded the corner. I never knew the names of all who had a word with me as I stood there at the crossing.

'Isn't it a shame, Hazel. Mrs Vigrass has had to be admitted to the Infirmary. Cancer.'

Mrs Vigrass and I used to take our children down to school when they started in the infants' class. We conjectured about them endlessly. Would they pass the eleven-plus? Who would they marry? We couldn't imagine ourselves actually becoming grandparents, maybe in thirty years' time, or less. Never did we consider ourselves mortal, that one day we may become ill – and die. How delightful those chats with Mrs Vigrass had been. It didn't seem possible. Why, she was only the same age as me. A cloud seemed to have crossed the sky. Life didn't seem at all fair. Now she would never know the answer to those questions, while I probably would. And how would her husband cope with a young son and daughter to bring up by himself? Well, he was having to manage already – she was away from home as it was.

Some days on the crossing the world seemed overwhelmed with trouble and tragedy, especially as the year drew to its close and the air became chill, and nights were dark. In the dying of the year one seems to emphasise the other, and I found myself already longing for the first signs of spring, even though winter itself had not begun. No sun, no warmth – nearly November.

Cats are luckiest of all, I think, when autumn and winter comes. Not, of course, strays, but family pets. They have no need to haul out shopping baskets and trek through blizzards to shops for their food and drink. Oh no. They can sprawl before a blazing fire, on a rug or armchair, while the milkman's hands become red with cold as he delivers icy-cold bottles to doorsteps, and while I had to carry heavy tins of cat food back to the Greedy Recipient. 'Miaow, what kind have you brought me?'

One late-October Saturday, as I set out for the shops after cooking breakfast, feeding Prince, making beds and coaxing a reluctant fire into a blaze, a gust of wind and rain lashed my face when I opened the door. I turned to look at the scene within. Prince, all twenty-seven stripes of her – I counted them once – was stretched full length on the rug. Roddy, her bosom pal from the bungalow opposite, was curled contentedly on blankets in the doll's pram in the corner of the room. My husband, pretending to be weighing up the pros and cons of central heating from the latest literature, which was a waste of time because we couldn't afford it anyway, had already closed his eyes in the armchair in a Saturday rapture, gentle snores emanating from his open mouth. Elizabeth and Caroline played cards before the fire. But I was glad. They were all there, healthy, if impoverished. They were there – and so would I be after I'd done the shopping.

That's another thing I was glad about being a Lollipop Lady. I heard about the trials and tragedies of others, and thanked God for the blessings I had. I had someone to work for, an aim in life.

14

Waifs and strays

Monday 24 October dawned sunny and fine, but it was bitterly cold on the first session of the week. A bus conductor leaned out to help a small tear-stained boy down the steps. He'd only be about five or six, and tears almost froze on his reddened cheeks as they cascaded down.

'Lollipop!' bawled the young conductor. 'Tell 'im where t'Catholic school is. Ah don't know.'

Well, I wasn't sure either, as mostly Protestant children went across to the local school. The child's bewildered face gazed up at me beseechingly. The little chap hadn't any gloves on, and was manfully trying to keep his fingers warm by plunging them deep into his trouser pockets.

'Haven't you any gloves, love?' I asked gently. He shook his head, gloves being apparently of little consequence. He sniffed, rubbing his nose on his sleeve. I handed him a paper tissue. He accepted it gratefully.

'Thanks, missus. Me muvver's gone to work – said there'd be plenty more on the bus – but there's only me.' He gave a great sobbing gulp.

At that moment four other children who attended the Catholic school sauntered round the corner. I sighed with relief.

'Oh, here's Martin. You'll take him safely there won't you, Martin?'

'Aye, sure.' Martin took the smaller boy's hand. The eldest of five brothers and sisters, he was used to assuming responsibility.

'All keep with me,' he commanded, 'and behave!'

The others lined up dutifully, and I asked the small stranger his name. 'Haven't you been to school before?'

'Me name's Patrick. We've just moved up 'ere.'

The road was clear. 'Come along then everybody, off to St Joseph's. And I'll bring a pair of gloves for you tomorrow, Patrick,' I promised. There were plenty of outgrown if not outworn ones at home.

When I saw children such as Patrick having to fend for themselves at such an early age it made me furious. Surely a mother's first consideration should be the welfare of her children? Why have them if they can't look after them – at least introduce them gently to a new experience? Don't leave them on their own the very first day at a new school. As for what pittance the unqualified housewife earned from factory, shop or other unskilled job, they'd be almost as well off keeping the home fires burning and saving money doing their own baking, cooking cheaper but equally sustaining food, and making clothes for the family themselves. But even if bound to turn out to a full-time job, most employers would surely allow time for an important day in a child's life? On the crossing I often nearly cried when I saw little ones crying, so early in a cold morning as well.

Going home up the lane I came across a group of 'working mums' with haversacks filled with leaflets handed out by a lady supervisor in a car. We exchanged smiles, sensing a fraternity. Those women pushed leaflets through letterboxes from nine till four. I'd applied for a similar job, when the moneylenders threatened to engulf us. The hourly pay was 3s 9d, ridiculous remuneration when such inconveniences result – bad temper and tiredness at the end of the day, slogging round streets, up and down steps all day long, then still having to go home and do the shopping, cook a meal, maybe spend the evening catching up on household jobs. And how about the cost of footwear? Of course, some are lucky if a widowed Gran lives with the family. If she is active, she can be a godsend. Old Mrs Burrows was exactly that to her daughter. She was bringing the youngest grandchild up from school the other dinnertime.

'Where's Joanna?' I asked, not having seen the eldest girl for some days.

'Ay, lass, she's still measling,' she sighed deeply, yet obviously more than content in her important role of stand-in while mum was at work. How much better than an old person being ignored.

From three thirty to four thirty one afternoon my already hazardous occupation was complicated by a huge black dog. The poor creature had a bloody-looking gash on a foreleg, which obviously needed attention. Because no one else was about, he decided I'd be the one to help. Each time I crossed with a group of children, the dog crossed too, limping and leaving a trail of blood in our wake. Sometimes he sat in the middle of the road to lick his wound. Then the youngsters crowded round him, patting him in sympathy as traffic roared nearer. Many times my heart felt ready to leap into my mouth as Blackie, as I called him, strolled casually in front of a car or bus. I never saw him again, but prayed for his safety.

On Thursday the 27th everybody mourned. It was the mass funeral at Aberfan, Wales, for the children who had lost their lives in the shocking mud of the coal tip avalanche the previous Friday. All day as I ushered 'my' children across the road I thought of those others, and was depressed and sad, especially for their grieving parents.

'I think the school teachers who so often said "Be quiet" to those once chattering children will so wish to hear their lively voices again,' I said to those who stopped to talk. I thought it particularly tragic when one mother told how her little son wouldn't drag himself out of bed when she called him over and over again to go down for his breakfast.

'I clouted him and sent him to school without any breakfast to punish him,' she recalled.

It was unbearable seeing and hearing such stories on the news, let alone being one of those who was there. The little chap had gone to the doomed school crying – and that was the last his mother saw of him. How we should try, no matter how provoked, never to 'fall out' with those we love, for we never know if we will ever see them again in this life.

Next morning danger came snapping round the corner at me. Rover, the Alsatian I had watched grow from a fat, fluffy, playful puppy, rushed at me, barking and baring his teeth, and 'putting the wind up me' far more than all the speeding traffic combined. Luckily his owner had him on a lead. I love dogs, and usually the feeling has been reciprocated.

'Oh don't run away from him – Rover won't hurt anybody,' remonstrated his windswept owner. One can't really apply the description 'owner' to someone who is, quite obviously, owned by the dog. In Rover's present mood I thought discretion the better part of valour, vowing never to let him snuffle his long snout under my white Lollipop coat again.

Not long after I heard that Rover had bitten a child badly and had to be 'put down'. A friendly, tail-wagging little roly-poly mongrel eventually took the place of the pedigree, for which I was truly thankful.

The big black Labrador who tried to fill in time while his owners were at work appeared on the crossing. This time he decided that chasing motor bikes would be a marvellous way of passing the time and, maybe, he thought, protecting me.

He crouched by my side, a bit of a *One Man and His Dog* kind of thing. Only I wasn't a man and it was motor bikes not sheep that needed his attention. As each bike zoomed past he was after it like a shot, sometimes getting close enough to try and snap the rider's ankles, and creating complete mayhem as the rider tried to avoid both dog and other vehicles. Then he would come panting back to me for praise – or so he'd be thinking. Drops from his steaming pink tongue plopping on the pavement as he regained his breath for the next enemy.

I was so worried about his safety as the time drew near for me to put Lollipop down the snicket and go home. Then I remembered that a policeman who kept guard dogs lived at the bottom of the lane. Luckily he was at home when I called, and he said he'd see what he could do. Whatever he did do, I never saw the motor bike chaser again.

After a brief respite for autumn half term, the last lap was on before

Christmas. With all the children safely across, I popped into Nellie's shop for a few odds and ends.

'Me breasts will have to come off eventually, they're rotten,' she announced proudly. 'But since ah've bin working full time with plenty to occupy my mind, not just stuck at home worrying about me health, I've been much better.'

The postman came in as I was on my way out. 'Any chance of a sorting job at the GPO in the evenings?' I asked. 'I've been told some can "knock up" over twenty pounds in seven days in the week before Christmas.'

'Sorry love, I think they've enough Christmas casuals already.'

I consoled myself that maybe I'd earn a few guineas with writing to magazines about funny happenings on the crossing.

15

'Some folk get all the bad luck...'

*A*s a Lollipop Lady I had a grand view of all that went on, able to watch without looking as if I was being a nosey parker (which I am).

One damp, dreary November afternoon, the cortège of Mr Wibley drove slowly round the corner of the lane, passing me on the main road. His rheumaticky old wife, in sombre black, sat staring ahead in the front car, looking completely stunned. She and 'her Joe' had always been something of a kindly joke among neighbours up our lane – but a joke that ought to happen more often. For what married person would not secretly long to be still walking hand-in-hand with their husband or wife when well into their seventies? 'Love's old sweet dream' can be even sweeter than when young, and certainly more precious.

John the gardener paused by my side. Hands in pockets, shaking his head in sorrow, he stood bare-headed, flat cap held in respect.

'I don't know how she'll manage now – they were all the world to each other,' he sighed. 'From the practical side of it, too. Joe did all the shopping, kept the garden trim – fragrant with roses in summertime. He used to give his missus a bunch of flowers at their cottage door every Saturday, just as if they were courting. Bloody death – makes yer wonder...'

'Still, she does have two married sons and a daughter – all married, but they're always visiting. And little Whisky,' I added, recalling the small rough-haired mongrel that Mr and Mrs Wibley had thought the world of.

'Like all t'rest of us,' continued John, stamping out a cigarette on the pavement. 'We're bereaved, feel lost, but somehow everything gets done, everything falls into place – jobs done, if not by the same hands. And life goes on.'

Nevertheless I couldn't help feeling a lump in my throat at the knowledge that everything finally comes to a close. Then the funeral procession was lost to view amid the traffic and a laughing group of youngsters jostled on the pavement.

Poor Mrs Wibley. She'd have a sad Christmas that year, as would many others. I could hardly believe we were into November already, and I'd been working on the crossing since February!

The day finished on an optimistic note. Brown Grandad sauntered across from the post box at tea-time, grinning from ear to ear.

'Ah've just booked next year's summer holiday,' he bragged. 'Ah think ah'll still be here next summer – and I hope you will too, Hazel,' he added, giving me a hug.

Next morning I listened to a tale of woe. A thirty-ish young mother, taking her three sons to school, confided as we waited for an opening in the traffic that her husband had ditched her for his secretary.

'I'm not destitute, I have a car, a good allowance – but what's that when the love of your life has gone? The children are too young to leave, I can't always get a baby-sitter – but worst of all … I feel so unwanted…' She blew her nose, eyes watering. 'You're so lucky, having your husband, Hazel – money is nothing, it's love that makes life worth living, isn't it?'

Husbands, especially dads, make me terribly angry when they do such rotten things – throwing over their wives who have gone through the agony of childbirth for them, when a newer edition takes their fancy. Listening to the troubles of others did me good, in a way, and made me grateful for the blessings I had. We hadn't a car, our budget was tighter than tight, but at least we had each other, and wanted no other. I finished the crossing duty and strode up the lane determined not to nag about the moneylenders for at least twenty-four hours.

Still in a 'Good Wife' mood I decided we'd have a lovely meal at tea-time – chicken, with all the trimmings, anticipating Christmas a little. Besides, it was Thursday, wage morning. However, my bubbling mood of Goodwill to All Men soon changed to one of evil intent to the shopkeeper, who'd taken 13s 9d for the chicken, but not taken the feet off as I'd asked him to. Usually they were oven-ready, apart from taking the little bag of giblets out. I'd been talking, and not noticed the omission.

I stared in mounting revulsion at those upturned pink, claw-like feet, and didn't know what to do. How about asking the milkman if he'd hack them off for me? Or shut my eyes and hope for the best as I swung the carving knife in what I hoped was the right direction? Oh no, I couldn't! But if I waited until Granville came home there'd be no super meal with apple sauce, mustard sauce – really strong – stuffing and all the rest of it. We'd end up with fish fingers and cabbage from the garden again. There was nothing else for it but to shove the bird in the oven on low, feet and all.

Trouble, trouble, trouble. Next day on the crossing Colin, a handsome, fair-haired eight-year-old with round schoolboy knees, short pants and wide, innocent blue eyes, put in a belated appearance at half past one as I was about to take Lollipop across the road to the snicket.

'Crikey, you're late Colin!'

His mum, stern-faced, hands thrust deep into her no-nonsense tweed coat, brought up the rear.

'Aye, we are. I'm gonna tell his teacher about yon buggers who've been picking on our Colin again. He daren't come to school by himself now. It's a bit of a devil, I must say, at his age.'

Mother and son stamped off down the snicket, she full of purpose and determination, Colin casting pleading backward glances in my direction.

Two insolent-looking Secondary Modern lads accosted me in the middle of the crossing during the last session of the day. Cigarette ends drooped from each mouth – they'd probably rolled them, as tobacco was spilling out.

'Gorra match, Lollipop?' drawled one. He took a lot of convincing that I didn't smoke. 'Yer bound to smoke on this job – I mean, whadya do to keep yer nose end warm this ruddy weather?'

'Don't know about no smoking, Phil,' leered the other. 'She looks a bit of hot stuff to me. Fancy a quick grope behind t'snicket, Lollipop?' A few more garbled remarks in similar vein, then they were gone.

Suddenly, further down the main road, I became aware of what at first looked like a life-size rag doll flapping up and down on all fours near the kerb. A woman stooped over the now still, prostrate figure, stroking what I now realised was the girl's head. A police car screeched to the scene, followed by a raucous, hooting ambulance, blue lights flashing. This was all happening on Tom's patch, the other warden. Then a vicar went to the scene – I saw his white 'dog collar'.

My attention was then diverted by the main bulk of four o'clock schoolchildren clamouring for me to take them across the road, as the ambulance and police car went screaming past on their way to the Infirmary.

Not knowing the cause of the commotion, I walked up the lane mentally cursing whoever, or whatever, had been responsible for injuring the child.

News of the accident was in the evening paper. Patricia, one of a large family of children, eleven years old, had been walking down the steps of a double-decker bus when a pack of unruly lads had pushed her. She had fallen down the rest of the steps of the bus, which, fortunately, had been slowing down as it neared a fare stage. It hadn't been a motorist's fault after all. How true that most injuries can be avoided. Horseplay is the cause of much damage, and all the ensuing anxiety to relatives, besides pain to the victim. All could be avoided if everybody had a bit more courtesy, patience, and thoughtfulness for others, and didn't act the fool in potentially dangerous situations.

After tea next evening Elizabeth, Caroline and I took a few outgrown clothes along to Patricia's home for her younger sisters. We hadn't any spare money to give, but I did want to give tangible evidence of our concern. Patricia's mother, recovering from the shock of her eldest daughter's accident, invited us in.

With whoops of surprise and joy the young children ran off into a corner of the large, clean but shabby room to investigate the contents of the carrier bags, while Fluffy, a black and white common or garden cat stopped licking herself in amazement. Her little pink tongue stuck out in astonishment at the presence of strangers in the house, and she retained her erect position, tongue in its pink, near paralytic state of shock, until we left. She seemed to be saying, as she huddled against the old-fashioned black Yorkshire range, 'This is my home, and however shabby and poor we are, I like it. So there!'

Next morning the crossing was a veritable 'grapevine' for all that was going on. I heard that Patricia had mercifully only suffered bruising and shock and was to be discharged from the Infirmary next day.

A new supermarket had been built further down the road, which was to remain open for late-night shopping two nights a week. On Mischief Night, 4 November, we went to do the shopping and saw gangs of youths prowling up and down the lane, as well as the handsome policeman who had been with me on my first morning; he assured us that everything appeared to be orderly and quiet.

However, on reaching home, laden with weekend shopping, we found that our front door knob had been tied with string to the drainpipe. It took us ages to undo the knots. It was a fine night, or I'd have felt more enraged than ever. Our good humour was fully restored, however, after a comforting warm through by the glowing fire, and cheese and toast for supper.

We had a small bonfire in the back garden next evening, and a few fireworks. My mother was a guest of honour, watching from the dining-room with the curtains open. Grandad had stayed at home to watch the string of bonfires up the hillside overlooking the Colne Valley near where they lived. He had bronchitis, so bonfire smoke was a pleasure to be avoided that year.

Monday morning came again, typical of early November, with a slight fog that resembling a thin, watery grey blanket, followed by rain. In the bread shop after the first crossing, Mrs Wood was still full of Patricia's accident.

'Ee, some folk get all the bad luck,' she puffed, wrapping two wheatmeal loaves in crisp tissue paper. 'Poor Mrs Monks always used to pop in here on Saturday afternoons to buy ice-cream for the kiddies' tea-time treat. But now her husband has no overtime at t'mill she can't afford to get them any more. Then this to happen to Patricia. Isn't it a shame – and some take it as their right to have ice-cream every blessed day of the week. Makes me quite cross.'

'But if you can have something every day it isn't a treat any more, is it, Mrs Wood?' I said. 'How awful it must be to be a millionaire...' (What a hypocrite I am at times!)

Then I dashed up the lane for my coffee, wondering how I might be able to buy Mrs Monks's tea-time treat on Saturday, without it looking too much like charity. Why some crave ice-cream in November baffles me. Even schoolchildren, coming back from the swimming baths with still damp hair and chattering with cold teeth at dinnertime, said how they were looking forward to a hot meal. I wondered why hair-dryers couldn't be supplied at the Baths, because even wearing a bathing cap the hair gets wet.

Caroline went to bed at a reasonable hour for once, as she was due to take her first eleven-plus exam next morning. The day dawned bright and sunny. How I wanted her to pass!

I put on my navy beret and white coat, pulled on the navy gloves, and left her lots of instructions, having to be on the crossing first before any children arrived.

'Don't come out of the house too soon, or your fingers will be so cold and stiff you won't be able to write quickly. But don't be late. And don't forget some paper tissues. Most of all, good luck!' A quick kiss, eyes filling with tears, then I ran down the lane.

On the crossing I became more and more agitated as one child after another came round the corner. Where was she? Surely everyone who was going to school had gone down the snicket by now? What if she'd fallen downstairs? Or couldn't lock the door? Had a piece of coal fallen out of the fire? Had Prince scratched her eyes out? Heart thumping madly, I looked up and down the lane, holding Lollipop, umpteen times, willing her to appear. This was the worst of being a working mother, feeling as though I ought to be split in two – one half to concentrate on the job that provided the money, the other half to stay at home and make sure instructions were carried out to the letter, especially on important eleven-plus mornings.

'Dear God, please let Caroline pass the eleven-plus,' was my silent prayer as I stood on the crossing. I wanted her to attend the same Girls High School I had. In my mind's eye I pictured her wearing the smart navy gym tunic with velvet yoke, the blue and white 'butcher boy' long-sleeved blouse, and navy and blue striped blazer in summer. There were such a lot of rough types at the Secondary Modern – boys could be bad enough bullies in Junior and even Infant School, but they'd be worse as they became teenagers.

Doubts assailed me yet again. Where was she? I stepped out into the lane and stared up it. Not a sign of her. Now it was almost a quarter to nine, and the exam would be starting soon. Caroline had been in the 'A' stream, but what if she missed the exam now, because of me not being there to see to whatever was delaying her? More than once I wildly thought about throwing Lollipop down and racing up the lane. I even considered packing the job in when it created all this anxiety. Then I thought how delightful it would be to watch the mounting excitement of the infants as Christmas drew near. Again I stepped into the road and peered up the lane, panic mounting second by second. Oh God, what should I do? Ask a passer-by to see to the children while I ran up home?

Oh, at last! It was Caroline, in her green winter coat and fluffy white scarf. Doing my best to calm down – after all, the last thing I wanted to do was upset her and ruin her chances – I tried to appear composed and smiling as she walked up to me. Sarah, from the bungalow opposite, was with her.

'Oh, thank God you're here!' I gasped, clutching her hand. 'Where have you been? All the others went down long since.'

A look of sheer exasperation flitted across my younger daughter's face.

'Mummy! You told me not to come down too early – you said my fingers would be too stiff for the exam. Now didn't you?'

We all laughed and I waved goodbye and good luck, breathing a silent prayer for her success, till they turned the corner down the snicket. Strange, isn't it, when you think that the Lollipop Lady you see apparently standing thinking about nothing in particular can be mentally down on her knees saying prayers or anything? What a good job our thoughts aren't transparent, or some motorists and thoughtless pedestrians would receive awful shocks. Imagine, thinking something vulgar or insulting about someone, with the words flickering beneath the 'STOP – CHILDREN' on Lollipop! 'What the hell are you doing, you silly moo?' aimed at a reckless female driver; unmentionable curses to the youth who, bent on catching a bus, hurtles across the crossing, thus encouraging children to follow. I'm sure if thoughts were translated into words on the lollipop sign I'd have been imprisoned for bad language many a time.

Perhaps because dads know it's not their traditional role to look after children besides a job, they don't seem to suffer from nervous exhaustion as much as working mothers. No wonder language is not always ladylike, to say the least!

My mind switched off from Caroline and her examination as I spied a bent old man who could hardly manage to totter. School Crossing Warden rules state that the sign must only be used for escorting children, but surely, I thought, it's only ordinary humanity to help such a pathetic figure. He reminded me of how the 'Dying Year' was portrayed, with his smudgy blue stubble casting a greyness round his chin, and faded watery eyes staring vacantly ahead before vacantly focusing, unsmiling, on me – perhaps unseeing, and lost in a vanished dream world of his own.

Had this broken-down relic ever been someone's lover? Someone's happy-go-lucky daddy, or Important Man of Business? Probably. As a passer-by remarked, 'What a shame for old Mr Lawrence. Such a smart, upstanding chap at one time!'

I started thinking that in some distant year, in the 21st century maybe, when I myself was bent and spent, physically as well as mentally, would some robot crossing warden ruminate in his computer brain, 'Dear me, to think I replaced a worn-out old hag like her…'?

But enough of such thoughts. My body was healthy and young. I could still laugh off those adverts offering hope to the over-fifties, even the over-forties. Vigorously, thankful for my present health (and that Caroline had turned up), I bounced back up the lane for my fortifying cup of coffee, the only forty-ish thing I wanted to know about, then went quickly upstairs to make the beds. I gazed out of the windows as my hands pulled the blankets into place. It was still 1966. Not 2006…

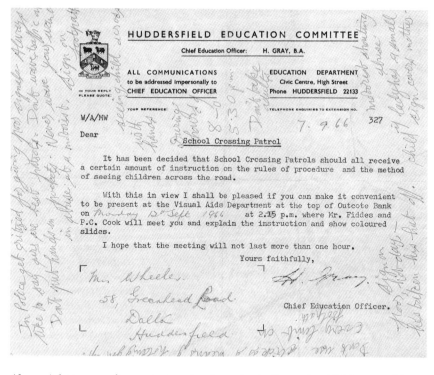

Above A letter regarding an instructional meeting in September 1966, covered in my scribbled notes taken during the session.

Below The school holiday schedule for 1966/67.

SCHOOL CROSSING PATROLS

Holiday Schedule for School year 1966-67

	Schools (Non R.C.)		Schools (R.C. only)
FIRST TERM		**FIRST TERM**	
Begins	Wed. Sept. 7	Begins	Wed. Sept. 7
Half Term	(Mon. Oct. 31 (Tues. Nov. 1	Half Term	(Mon. Oct. 31 (Tues. Nov. 1
Ends	Thurs. Dec. 22	Ends	Thurs. Dec. 22
SECOND TERM		**SECOND TERM**	
Begins	Tues. Jan. 10	Begins	Tues. Jan. 10
Half Term	(Mon. Feb. 13 (Tues. Feb. 14	Half Term	Mon. Feb. 13
Ends	Wed. March 22	Ends	Wed. March 22
THIRD TERM		**THIRD TERM**	
Begins	Tues. April 11	Begins	Mon. April 10
Polling Day	Thurs. May 11	Religious Holiday	Thurs. May 4
Whit	May 29 – June 2	" "	Thurs. May 25
		Whit	May 29 – June 2
Ends	Thurs. July 20	Religious Holiday	Thurs. June 29
		Ends	Thurs. July 20

Left The view from our house in Greenhead Lane, Dalton, Huddersfield. On the left is one of the entrances to 'Oaklands', then an Old People's Home.

Below At the bottom of Greenhead Lane (in the background), on the main Wakefield Road, was 'my' crossing, seen here being manned by my successor, in full 'barrage balloon' uniform! The road was certainly not often as quiet as this scene suggests!

Above Looking down Wakefield Road from the corner of Greenhead Lane in 1966, with a Dodge lorry having turned from Dalton Green Lane towards the crossing, to be followed by a motorbike and a Ford Anglia. Note the overhead trolleybus wires.

Right Another view of the same junction. Note the tower wagon parked on the right, being used to repaint the lamp post (see overleaf). A No 73 bus is in the distance.

Left The lamp post painter at work, with his canine 'mate'.

Below The Belisha beacons and bollards on the crossing were also regularly maintained. Behind the cleaner is Nellie's shop, and beside it the snicket where Lollipop was 'garaged' when not in use.

Below My wage slip for 3 July 1966, showing the standard weekly rate of £3 14s 6d.

●	1 2 4 7	29	1	1 5	N C			Graduated Nat. In
	1 2 4 7	29			Name		3 JUL 66	Sick or Social
	1 2 4 7	29	WHEELER H					Savings
●	1 2 4 7	29						

Above Some of my 'customers' posed with me against the stone wall on the corner of Greenhead Lane. I am in my summer uniform, Sarah Venables is on the left, next to Caroline, and Mrs Dalby is standing on the right.

Below Halfway across! I'm holding Caroline's hand. On the right, next door to Smith's, is a fish and chip shop.

Income Tax			GROSS WAGE	3. 15. 0 + ●
Nat. Insce. Council's Cont.		11. 4 −	Nat. Insce. Employee's Cont.	6 −
Rents			Superannuation	
Subs./ Pay Offs			AMOUNT DUE	3. 14. 6 + ●

Taking Caroline across.

Katherine Abbot waiting to cross at the end of the summer term, laden with typical games of the period (which she dropped halfway across!).

Looking after his sister: two more 'customers' in characteristic 1960s duffle-coats wait for me to take them across, while Mrs Moorhouse waits for a bus.

Above and left More Juniors near the crossing in the summer of 1966 (Caroline is enjoying a lollipop). Wood's bread shop has its blind down against the sun. Between it and the fish shop is where Brown Grandad used to pursue Beverley through the hanging washing!

Left Their destination, Dalton Junior School.

The girls: Caroline (*left*) on her way home from school in 1966, still enjoying that lollipop, and Elizabeth, aged 10 in 1964, as a member of Huddersfield Primary Youth Orchestra, practising in the garden at home.

Below Shampoo time for the dolls in the back garden at Greenhead Lane.

Blackpool, late summer 1966. During our none-too-successful weekend away, my husband Granville poses with Caroline (left) and Elizabeth and some of the famous Illuminations. The theme was Christmas characters. Christmas *crackers* more exemplified our lives at that time!

Caroline, braving the
elements on horseback.

Below Granville on the 'prom'.

Top and above Our cat Prince investigates Caroline's toy horse transporter, and poses beside her 'dog on wheels' in the back garden.

Left 'Who goes there?' I won a prize in a magazine competition with this picture of Roddy, Prince's friend from the bungalow opposite.

Above Granville and Tiny, the donkey that belonged to a Children's Home at Almondbury, near Huddersfield.

Right Caroline in Greenhead Lane with the policeman who first introduced me to the 'Lollipop Beat', and one of my canine 'customers', who regularly crossed with me.

Above The lodge to 'Oaklands'. A friend of ours, Mrs Richardson, lived there, and claimed that it was haunted.

Below Elizabeth and Diane, the daughters of our Hungarian friends, pose with Sarah Venables (centre) in the grounds of 'Oaklands', with Prince behind them.

Opposite above Harry Barrowclough, who looked after the gardens of 'Oaklands' Old People's Home (and was everybody's heart-throb), attends to a wall in the grounds. Behind him is Greenhead Lane, while in the background is Greenhead Avenue. Our house was a few doors up the lane.

Right Harry, ever helpful and cheerful, at work in the lovely gardens at 'Oaklands'.

Fishing in the 'tadpole swamp' in a field beside 'Oaklands', a favourite hunting ground for little boys on their way to and from school. Unfortunately the swamp sometimes yielded frogs, and on one memorable occasion a boy on my crossing slipped one into my wellingtons!

16

Windy, itchy weather

Two old ladies from 'Oaklands', the big stone house opposite, strolled arm in arm through the damp November leaves. One was tallish, wearing thick grey stockings and a well-worn black coat and thick grey hair an exact match for her stockings, sallow complexioned, and dark sallow round her eyes. She looked an odd choice of companion for the frail, bird-like, dainty little lady leaning so trustingly on her arm. Yet what a picture of tranquillity they made as they moved haltingly together in the early morning.

I thanked God that all women with cars and a Top Job were not as autocratic as the one who annoyed me before eight-thirty one morning. My (to her) menial job began then, and not a minute before if I did not choose to be there earlier.

So what right had Madam, transporting her three mincing Little Dears in precise schoolboy caps (they attended the small Private School at the top of the lane), to beckon imperiously to me at eight twenty-five. If she wished to get to her job early, couldn't she raise her expensively suited posterior and escort the boys herself?

Too angry to say 'Good morning' – it was still not officially time for me to begin – I crossed, picked Lollipop up from its resting place down the snicket and attended to the mute small boys in their brown uniforms while their mother, without so much as a smile or word of thanks, zoomed off up the road. People like her made me want to give my notice in there and then. She probably thought that a mere Lollipop Lady was there just for her convenience. In any case, it was a job any fool could do. But I reckoned I was far better tempered and in far better health with my lowly open-air job than she would be at the end of her day, shut in her centrally heated office with shrilling telephones and irritable boss.

Fortunately, for the rest of the day, my equanimity was more than restored by a gentleman who worked in a fish shop in town, and stopped to have a word with me.

'Do you know, lass,' patting me gently on my back, 'd'you know, tha's got a reet good name round here for seeing t'kids across safely. Everyone trusts you and your judgement completely. Ah'm very grateful to thee.'

His son Roger was one of my regular 'customers'. I smiled with pleasure, dismissing the Imperious Madam from my mind as so much junk, while the fish man's words kept my spirit soaring joyfully to face whatever else the day might bring.

Some little realise the devastating effect that words and actions have on their fellow men and women. Everyone ought to keep a safety belt on their tongues as well as on their bodies. A hasty word, and the victim's mind is solely on that, and not on what is happening round about.

It wasn't a person who worried me next day, a cold, bright blue and gold 10 November. After the first crossing of the day, back home I always opened the living room window to let in Roddy, the bungalow cat, to share warm milk with Prince. That morning there weren't two cats waiting on the window sill, but three. The third – skinny, miserable-looking, big eyes gazing out of dull black fur – was poor old Sooty who used to live next door before his owners moved to another district.

'Sooty, come on love, come inside.' I tried to coax him in with the other two, but he was too timid, yet crying and pawing the cold window as he stared dolefully in, watching Prince and Roddy slobbering up the dishes of milk left over from my coffee. Occasionally I saw the children who used to live next door, and told them that Sooty was still hanging about. Half-hearted attempts were made at intervals to capture the scrawny cat and take it to the new home, but Sooty always came back, looking more miserable and dejected than before.

When Sooty was miserable, I was miserable. Unable to coax him inside the warm room, I took some milk outside, accompanied by jealous hissing from Prince and Roddy, safe on Home Ground. The wind howled round and I often cried for all the other helpless creatures in similar predicaments. Would any cat *choose* to sit on a cold outside window sill, with snow falling all around? Would a person? Do as you would be done by.

I couldn't go back to the crossing without trying to help Sooty, so I telephoned the RSPCA. What a shock – what an attitude the man at the other end of the line had!

'All we are concerned with is cruelty, madam. Why not capture the cat then contact the owners?'

'I can't do that. Our cat won't tolerate a strange one in the same room,' I replied desperately, watching Sooty shivering in a corner of the window sill.

'You have another room, haven't you?'

I could picture the scene – a frenzied Sooty, let loose in the front room, charging up curtains, racing along the mantelpiece... Besides, how to contact the people who owned him? The dad was at work all day, and they weren't on the telephone. I explained all that to the imperious voice at the other end.

'Well, all I can suggest then is don't feed it and it will go away.'

'Oh, you callous devil!' I snarled, slamming the receiver down. I'd achieved nothing, only wasted time and money. He had also intimated that if Sooty's owners didn't give their authority for him to be put to sleep – surely a better fate than starving to death in a bitter Yorkshire winter – then the RSPCA could do nothing.

Three months had slipped by since Sooty's owners left. Surely that spoke for itself – they weren't concerned about Sooty's fate. At the crossing I kept hoping to see one of the family, but no luck, so I gave a message to a little girl who was in the same class as Maureen. I scribbled on a piece of paper, 'Your Starving Cat Sooty Needs You.'

Nothing happened. Sooty kept appearing on the window sill. One morning my neck and even my teeth seemed to ache with the bitter blasts as I stood, pacing up and down every now and again in an effort to keep warm. But the cold morning was obviously keeping everyone at home till the last minute, except Madam and her three private schoolboy sons between eight thirty and eight forty-five.

Stepping into the end of the lane to look hopefully for signs of life didn't have much benefit on my circulation. If I'd dared, I might have risked a solo 'twist' session, or had a go at reviving my tango days, with the Crossing Pole as partner. Knowing all too well what it was like, feeling the intense cold, helpless to even keep myself warm, gave me a deep affinity with Sooty and others like him. A rich man can never understand a poor one if he's never been poor himself. You've to be in the other one's shoes – or in this case, paws – to fully understand the depth of misery. Going home to a roaring fire after shivering on a slow morning at the crossing, then seeing poor Sooty, who couldn't hope to sit before a fire all day – and all night too – made every fibre of my being ache to relieve his suffering. But how?

Christmas was beginning to steal into the atmosphere, into conversations and, tangibly, into the shops, emphasising the sadness of those to whom the season spells only misery. Hard up as we were all the time, I could never steel myself to say to Elizabeth and Caroline, 'We're not bothering with toys this year. Wouldn't clothes be better?' – something they needed.

Granville suggested saying that at their age it's a bit silly to hang stockings up. But no, as long as ever they found pleasure in childish things I'd contrive to fill their stockings on Christmas Eve. Childhood vanishes all too soon.

So when ten- and twelve-year-old hands dragged me eagerly to window-shop, go inside, look at games, and try out musical teddy bears, admire beautiful dolls with flaxen curls, and stick-like teenage dolls with more clothes in their wardrobe than we could dream of having ourselves, I was a willing companion. Even at my age, I still think there's no thrill like gazing at brand new dolls and teddies, while carols tinkle in the background in the weeks leading up to Christmas.

On Monday I had an awful pain in the back of my neck, and knew that if I stood there in the freezing cold it would only make it worse, and take longer to get better. I telephoned the police in plenty of time to say I couldn't go to the crossing and could they please put a replacement there.

It proved how important Lollipop people are: the morning was only slightly advanced when I glanced out to see Mr Fiddes bounding up the garden path. He was in charge of crossing patrols.

'I'm so sorry you're not up to the mark Hazel, but we can't do without you for long – indeed, you're almost indispensable.'

'I can still manage to make a cup of coffee and home-made cakes,' I grinned, but held my neck stiffly so he'd see I wasn't kidding about my condition.

'We can't get reliefs for love nor money,' he sighed, sipping the freshly ground coffee appreciatively. 'Police have to take over when our Lollipops are ill – and they're overworked as it is.'

Accompanying him stiffly to the door, I must have looked like one of those wooden Russian dolls, with an old multi-coloured scarf wound round my immobile neck and smelling of Vick rub, with which I'd smothered my upper regions that morning. But I still loved playing the heroine.

'Yes, yes, I promise. I'll be on the crossing first thing tomorrow morning,' I assured him.

How I wished I hadn't been so impulsive with my promises when the morning came! My neck was still aching and rain was pelting down heavily, seemingly non-stop. Even a thick scarf, tucked into my waterproof coat, and an upturned collar proved useless against the relentless, blinding rain. It found its way down my neck, trickling remorselessly on. It seeped into my wellingtons. I was soaked through on all four crossing times, with no time for my equipment to dry out in between.

And I was still so worried about Sooty. There he crouched, on such a vile day, not fit to turn a Lollipop Lady out into, let alone a dog, or poor Sooty.

'What an awful day for stray animals,' I remarked to a lady waiting for the bus into town.

'Oh, I don't worry about those,' she shrugged. 'They've got fur coats on, they're all right.'

Oh, I was blazing mad – hopping, hopping mad when people are as insensitive as that. As long as they were OK it didn't matter a damn about anyone or anything else. She boarded the bus, and I stuck my tongue out at her when she had her back to me. Swine!

Another person came up, so I tried him out.

'Isn't it terrible for stray animals on a day like this?' I said.

'I'll say,' the old chap nodded. 'Bare paws on slushy, ice-covered roads – and those poor devils who've been in fights and have patches of fur ripped off. What a ruddy life for some poor buggers.' I could almost touch the empathy between us.

'Naked skin open to the frost,' I commiserated.

'All we can do, Lollipop, is say a prayer for 'em. I know I do. So long.'

As he left me, I blew him a kiss, which he returned. And for a moment the sun broke through the leaden skies.

When at last the soakings of the day were over, my mind turned to another kind of soaking – in a hot bath, with a treat of salts and bubble bath oil left over from last Christmas. Relaxed and soaking away the cares of the day in scented hot water, my faith in human nature could be restored. Maybe tomorrow the sun would shine, birds would sing, and every animal in the world would awake to find itself sheltered, fed, loved, and wanted. I yearned to wash the troubles of the day down the plughole along with the muck!

I couldn't wait to get into that fairyland of escape, so I sped upstairs that dreary November evening, anticipating a hot bath, supper, then to bed with a magazine or book. Singing in joyous anticipation, I ran up the stairs two at a time, into my dressing-gown, and turned the hot tap on. No! Cold. Stone, stone cold. Yet the fire had been on all day – we had no immersion heater, so it was that or nothing. I put my hands on the cylinder in sheer disbelief. Cold as Christmas. I leaned over the banister.

'Who – who left the hot water tap running?' As expected, silence. Mr Nobody had been at work again.

So bed and oblivion, with aching neck and muscles, which I'd hoped the hot water might relax away, could not come too soon that night.

Mid-November continued wild and wet. One of the silliest garments for anyone, let alone a child, was the waist-length anorak. It was serviceable to the waist, especially those with hoods, but the lower extremities were exposed to the elements. I recalled the sensible, full-length gabardines I had worn in winter at the Girls High School, and the navy felt hat with school-colours hatband, fitting snugly with an elastic band beneath the chin to keep it on in the windiest of weathers. Yet in the 'sixties, fashion was the priority, not common sense.

A number of wet, unhappy little Infant School children were sniffling and sobbing as they appeared in bedraggled groups at half past three. Rain was lashing down, yet a few still only wore thin summer dresses beneath anoraks, which, sodden through, clung to bare, reddened knees and flapped miserably in the biting wind.

'Don't worry, pet, you'll soon be home by a lovely warm fire,' I comforted them.

One little fellow, trying manfully to hang on to an armful of crayoned papers, lost his cap a couple of times when it was hurled into the air by a roguish wind. Why couldn't drawings and those huge cornflake-packets-cum-sailing-boats and goodness knows what be kept at school till another day, when it was obvious that they'd be soaked and ruined almost before they were out of the school yard?

Gardener John doffed his wet cap to me in passing. Grinning cheerfully, with raindrops plopping off his nose end, he appeared to be the only cheerful person I'd seen that day. When I said so, John smiled knowingly, and winked.

'Ah knows how to carry on, Lollipop. Ah've been asleep in my hut by a roaring fire all t'time this lot's been going on. Ah used me brains and stayed put. So tha sees, it's just a case of being in t'reet place at t'reet time. Ah'm off home now, for me tea – after a hard day's work,' he laughed.

Black clouds gathered again while huge drops of rain ran coldly down my face. A thin, weary-looking young woman rushed round the corner pushing a pram.

'Keep an eye on it for me, will yer luv, till ah nip in t'shop?' she pleaded. 'Don't let it be blown over with this ruddy wind, will yer? Ee, thanks, Lollipop.'

Oh for an extra pair of eyes and arms to meet all the requests I received on the 'Lollipop Beat'! But it was good to know I was of use in the world. And the feedback from grateful harassed passers-by was lovely too.

Only drunkards and heavy sleepers probably managed to sleep that night. Dustbin lids were hurled through the air by a gale-force wind to come to rest with a metallic clang in somebody else's garden. Our garden hut door, usually tightly closed, with a stone shoved by it for extra security, sprang open, bang, bang, banging hour after hour. You know how it is, you think that will be the last time – so why get out of a warm bed? But it keeps on throughout the long windy night.

There is purpose even in such wild nights as those. Neighbours who hadn't spoken for months over some triviality or other, now had to be humble and charming in order to retrieve belongings the next morning. Long-since-frozen faces of enmity cracked into thank-you smiles as dustbin lids were handed back over suburban fences. Even the odd pair of muddied Y-fronts was seen to be handed back over a fence.

What a clean, bright blue and gold morning it dawned after the storm. Everything was washed clean and the air was intoxicatingly fresh as I

swung down the lane at eight twenty-five. But the giddy wind was far
from entirely subdued, even though the rain had rained itself out.

My navy beret was whipped from my head many times, leaving my hair
criss-crossed over my eyes like a wet, bedraggled Dulux dog. I was so fed
up chasing it in front of cars and buses that I rammed it into my shopping
bag for safety. Even the bag had to be wedged in the furthest corner of
Nellie's shop doorway, held down with a stone to stop the wind stealing
that as well.

The high wind lifted skirts, hats and hair as it blustered into every nook
and cranny. It blew old Mrs Pritchard across my path as she lurched
forward to catch her breath and to talk with me. Something had triggered
off memories of the 1930s.

'Whew!' she panted, re-tying a plastic rainhood under her chin. 'It was
a day like this when my husband and son were carted off to hospital with
scarlet fever back in the 'thirties.' She leaned on her stick, eyes awash
with memories. She didn't see a Lollipop Lady then, but a young man and
his son who meant so much to her even now. 'D'you know, when they
came home my son was absolutely lousy. *Lousy!*' she shouted above the
howling wind. 'I'd to take t'lad to t'barber's straightway to have all his
hair cut off. Ee, poor little sod looked like a ruddy hard-boiled egg when
t'chap had finished with him. Then he'd to rub special ointment on his
scalp. Then, would you believe it, when Fred came home from work next
day he said he felt wick too. Scratch, scratch, bloody well scratch. So ah
dowsed his head wi' ointment as well. Awful stink it had, but ah didn't
care whether he had to go to work or not – ah wasn't having him giving
me the buggers too.'

Mrs Pritchard scratched her grey hair beneath the plastic hood. 'Fair
makes me itch this wind. Don't it you? Anyway, be seeing yer – so long.'

My mind flashed back to those nit-ridden days of the 'thirties, and I
wondered where all the nits had gone. Someone wrote a song: 'Where do
all the flies go in wintertime?' I toyed with the idea of making a fortune
with a song entitled 'Where have all the nits gone in the 'sixties?'

A child used to sit in the desk in front of me at what was then known
as the Council School, before I passed the eleven-plus to transfer to the
High School. Dorothy had bright ginger hair. How I managed to pass the
exam with the flea circus performing in the desk nearby I'll never know.
When the children ran out of the snicket I watched the ginger-headed
ones in particular – why was it usually *ginger* hair that nits seemed to
prefer? I'd have been wary about marrying a ginger-haired man!

17
Deadlock on the crossing

Christmas had been spoiled, to my mind, by trying to update it, to commercialise the festival. In town, after queuing for my wages at the Education Department with other Lollipop people, I was idling round the shops, thinking about buying presents, when I saw one of those Father Christmas Grottos in the toy department of a big store. What a disappointment when I saw who was dishing out the half-crown parcels. Not the beloved, bewhiskered Santa of my childhood, but a black-masked, thick-thighed Batman in sexy black tight trousers! Horrid! I knew where not to take my two if they felt they were still young enough to pay Santa a pre-Christmas visit.

Returning home after the day's work was over, I caught up with poor old Mrs Wibley, whose husband had died a few weeks earlier, toiling up the lane alone. Mother was at our house, so I invited Mrs Wibley in to meet her. Both widows now, I hoped they might find common ground for conversation.

'I kept my Joe in the house with me right up to the funeral,' Mrs Wibley faltered, wiping a tear from her eye as I put the kettle on. 'I loved him far too much to send him to one of those funeral homes.'

'I should think so,' sympathised mother, who in 1969, three years later, sold my stepfather's bed and gave his clothes away before he'd even died. He had terminal cancer, so it wasn't a callous act. Mother was kindness itself to everybody. But she did panic. She had experienced being widowed, so understood.

Both sipped tea and nibbled newly baked cherry buns while Mrs Wibley, emboldened by this obvious empathy with my mother, continued tearfully, 'And do you know, our little Whisky licked my Joe's cold face as he lay in his coffin in the front room. I'd a right job trying to get him away. He nipped inside the coffin and snuggled into the white laying-out sheet to be near him.'

Mother sympathised and offered another cherry bun. It called for more than a cup of tea, so I brought out the brandy bottle, kept strictly for emergencies – and this was one. All three of us were in a state of emotional collapse – the two older ones because Mrs Wibley was newly widowed, Mother had been widowed on the eve of her Silver Wedding in 1948, marrying again seven weeks later (and widowed again in 1969), and me because I couldn't even contemplate being alone.

Later I walked the old lady up the lane to her cottage, it then being quite dark, and waited until she opened the door and switched on the light, to be greeted wildly by an ecstatic Whisky. In his excitement at his mistress's return he leaped up and down, giving indiscriminate licks at both our faces.

Despite her seventy-odd years, and the additional handicap of a bad leg – she'd fallen and broken it two years earlier – she went through the ritual of giving Whisky her glove, stooping low to hand it to the little dog so he could bear it in triumph to the front room. Whisky held his head high, and we two followed, like bridesmaids to the altar.

Walking back down the lane, I thanked God that *I* was not a widow – I couldn't change a light bulb or deal with a mouse or wasp – or moneylenders!

One of the disadvantages of being in the same place, at the same time, five days a week, is that everyone knows where to contact you. It was a good job my face wasn't on posters for a robbery or a murder. I felt ill at ease, to put it mildly, when a car slowed to a standstill and out of it briskly stepped the new Junior School headmaster. I felt the colour mounting guiltily into my face. It had been all right writing those high-handed notes to him from the anonymity and safety of my home, but now what to say…? He strode up to me with a determined expression on his middle-aged countenance, and I forced a wan smile, desperately trying to recall what I'd written in those frequent notes I'd sent him. 'Dear Sir, please excuse Caroline from going to the swimming baths.' She hated the smell of them let alone being pushed around in the water by boisterous lads.

I'd hated swimming lessons too, ever since having to kneel at the side waiting for the butch, ginger-haired instructress to push us all in, one after the other. My big toe had caught in the pipe, and I'd been stuck, face down. Hell – sheer hell. So I willingly wrote those letters, asking for Caroline to be excused. We weren't likely to be going on long expensive sea voyages in any case, so why bother…?

Oh dear, those excuses. 'Caroline has a cold.' 'Caroline gets spots after going to the baths. The doctor says she is probably allergic to the chlorine.' 'Dear Mr – I do not wish my daughter to attend swimming baths as she is extremely nervous…' Now the recipient of those notes – written in the aggressiveness of the moment, with time and space twixt writer and recipient – was standing before me, ready for a head-on clash.

He sized me up, head on one side, trying to match my writing to the person, I imagined.

'Mrs Wheeler?'

'Yes?' I tired to infuse brightness, alertness, and intelligence, plus plenty of determination, into that monosyllable. Really, he was quite a handsome, charming man! I smiled, half in a friendly manner, and half in what I hoped might be interpreted as a sexy manner (if anyone can look sexy in stub-toed wellingtons), daring him to utter anything I didn't agree with. Swimming baths *were* horrible.

He coughed. Nervously. 'Mrs Wheeler – Hazel – about Caroline not attending swimming lessons...' (I liked it when he called me Hazel – it sounded so much younger than 'Mrs'.) 'It's the apparent permanency of it all that bothers me, you see...'

'But wouldn't it be foolish, especially now the eleven-plus exams are in progress, for her to risk getting a cold, or spots, or one of those vile verrucas many get on their feet?'

My adversary was struck dumb. He scratched his head, not knowing how to answer the Lollipop Lady.

'Besides, as Caroline doesn't like water that much, except in a bath, I don't think she will ever put herself in a position where she might drown. In any case, personally I think I'd rather drown once by accident than be terrified once a week,' I concluded.

The Junior School headmaster shrugged and made no reply. I filled in the silence.

'I prefer her to pass the eleven-plus than have her wasting time shivering in the baths, scared to raise more than one leg off the ground. If she'd been going to swim, she'd have been swimming before now.' I was well into my stride. 'I've seen children travel home with wet hair many a time – children should have freedom of choice in these matters. Freedom to risk drowning if they wish to do so. But not be forced into something they dread, every week.'

Deadlock on the crossing. Headmaster and Lollipop Lady equally determined that their point of view was the correct one, yet both striving desperately to maintain the air of cordiality between them.

'It's the same with somersaults,' I went on. 'Why should any child have to live in fear of PE lessons, be compelled to do something they're afraid of? It does more harm than the exercise benefits them.'

Caroline once told me about the PE instructor making her try to do a handstand – he had held her by the ankles, upside down, and she had clutched his trousers legs while attempting to flounder about in the air, and both had collapsed in a heap, laughing.

Before going out to work I had always pushed confrontations with people in authority on to my husband. Now I realised I was quite enjoying the thrust and parry. I dug Lollipop obstinately into the pavement, as though it was a weapon – a bayonet, at the ready. I wasn't alone. I had Lollipop. I stared at him. He took out a handkerchief and wiped his forehead. Time was on my side. It was almost time for school to begin.

'Well, I do hope you will see my point of view,' was his parting shot.

'I do,' I replied. 'But I don't agree with it. Good afternoon.'

I determined to secure a doctor's note for Caroline, about her allergy to chlorine. A friend of hers, Judy, regularly had sore red eyes after going to the baths. Authorities don't treat children as individuals, but as one mass-produced group who have to conform to everything they say. It seemed to me that parents were fast losing the right to have any say over their children's well-being.

I went into Nellie's shop to tell her about the encounter when the crossing duty was over. She agreed with me.

'My eldest lad, poor kid, had all the others making fun of him because he's so fat. It isn't his fault. Just something that's physically wrong with him.' Nellie handed me a few biscuits. 'Take them back for your elevenses. All that teasing made him worse – he almost had a nervous breakdown. Kids used to give him hell when he had to strip for PE and at the blasted swimming baths.'

There's nothing like a bit of gossip for making a person feel justified. I told Nellie about when the PE instructor tipped Caroline upside down to try and make her do a handstand, and she'd grabbed his trouser legs, hanging on for grim death while he held her feet in the air.

'Lot of silly devils, some of 'em,' said Nellie, as we laughed at the memory of it.

She stubbed out her cigarette ferociously. 'Education authorities are constantly at me to force us to make Peter go to the baths and do PE, but I'm damned if I will. Tears and all the scenes aren't witnessed by those buggers, sitting smugly in their warm offices making rules for other people's children. OK, so most kids enjoy swimming and PE. But there's always the odd one or two that don't fit the pattern.'

I nibbled a biscuit. 'Have a swig of lemonade with it, Hazel.' Nellie poured some into a glass.

'The odd ones out should be given sympathy and understanding,' I said, 'not forced into doing something it's not in their nature to enjoy. Grown-ups aren't forced to do things. Children are human beings too, only smaller.'

That evening I telephoned the doctor to make an appointment, feeling quite indignant that after all that trailing up and down the lane during the day I'd to go out again during the evening. The trail should not have been necessary. I had won the battle. The doctor had no hesitation about scribbling a note to say that in his opinion Caroline was allergic to chlorine, and must not go swimming.

A vague depression came over me, despite the victory. It's not pleasant to be at cross-purposes with a child's teacher. But one must stand up for one's rights.

That weekend Mrs Vigrass succumbed to the cancer, dying after an operation failed to stop its spread. Now, I thought sadly, she will never know if Adrian does pass the eleven-plus.

Another thought struck me. How dreadful – the English paper was due to be taken the following Wednesday, the day his mother was to be cremated. Adrian was a clever, intelligent boy, yet I felt sure such a blow could lessen his chance of passing the exam. His sister had passed the eleven-plus two years before, and now went to the Girls High School.

How good it was to have a husband to talk to when hearing about tragedy.

'I wonder if the Education Authorities will make an exception if Adrian doesn't pass?' I asked Granville.

'Well, as he's in the "A" stream already, so they may consider his school work, and the present circumstances,' he replied.

I held his hand, tightly. Mr Vigrass had nobody's hand to hold that night, and I couldn't stop crying for him.

Monday 21 November turned out to be a cold sunny day, the kind of day that inspired me to dash round the house cleaning in preparation for next month's festivities – one of those 'get up and go' days.

At the midday crossing the chap arrived who cleaned the roadside equipment. Armed with buckets of hot, soapy water, and cloths of varying degrees of muckiness stuffed into pockets, which seemed to sprout out from all over his person. His expression was one of never-changing joviality, down to earth, content with his lowly status, envying no man.

'Afternoon, Lollipop!' he greeted me. 'Are you setting off for Christmas then?'

'Oh no, we can't afford,' I replied, returning his friendly smile.

'Ee, me and t'missus allus go to Blackpool. Can't afford any other holiday during t'year, but we prefer being away at Christmas. We've never been lucky enough to know how to get childer,' he continued, busily polishing the bollards in the middle of the road to a gleaming whiteness. 'So we've no need to stay at home.'

'Are there organised games at the hotel?' I wanted to know, as he mischievously pretended to polish my face.

'Wouldn't want 'em,' he snorted derisively. 'We goes to this same little spot every year, reet good digs. Let her know we'll be arriving on a Friday neet or whenever, and there's always a piping hot meat and taty pie waiting for us supper.'

'*Then* what do you do, Alf?

He roared with laughter, swishing a cloth across my rear. 'Whadya think? We play bingo, sup ale, an' listen to t'Salvation Army Band on t'North Pier.' He executed a little dance of gleeful anticipation, then picked up his bucket, winked, plonked a kiss on my face, and was off, whistling down the road to the next lot of bollards.

Next day matched my mood, a variable day of sunshine, dark cloud, rain, and bitter cold. A day was always off to a bad start when one of the family was out of sorts. Or pretended to be.

It was such a rush between seven and eight as it was, without having to bother with somebody who was ill – prising them from their beds, emptying cold hot-water bottles, feeding the cat, who was always there behind the living-room door waiting to trip the first one down – me.

Elizabeth was the cause of the disquiet, but I didn't know whether the headache was feigned because it was a maths morning.

'You'd better not go then,' I sighed, always giving the benefit of the doubt. I'd have felt such a monster making her go to school if she really did feel ill. But it was awful having to leave my wan-faced daughter, professing that all she wanted to do was go to sleep. Then, as soon as I was out of the gate and turned to look up at the bedroom window, the light was switched on. Elizabeth wanted to read the new copy of *Jackie* that had just been delivered through the letter box, the little demon! Annoying, but far better than her being ill.

At midday she sauntered down in her blue dressing-gown to curl up in front of the fire, now the threat of school and algebra was over, and happily thread a few more shiny emerald green raffia strands into a lampshade she was making for Grandma's Christmas present. Later, a fully-recovered-from-the-mystery-illness Elizabeth suggested baking ginger biscuits while I went to the last crossing duty of the day.

18

Prize-winners

Whenever I had to leave Elizabeth or Caroline alone in the house I was full of dos and don'ts. 'Don't open the door if anybody knocks.' 'Don't waft past the fire with your nightdress.' 'Don't put Prince's claws near your face.' 'Hold the banister when you are coming downstairs.' It was not half as relaxing going to the crossing when leaving them in the house, but at least I was very near. I could sprint up the lane in a minute or two if I heard a fire engine screaming up or down the lane! How some parents can go out leaving small children alone I'll never understand – I was anxious enough and they were nearly in their teens.

Adrian was back at school after the trauma of his mother's death. When I saw him coming down the lane I wondered whether to say anything about it. In the end I decided not to, and tried to get my feelings across by smiling extra understandingly, and ventured to hold his hand as we crossed, giving it a reassuring squeeze as I left him. Actions speak louder than words.

About a quarter past four his sister Jennifer came to the crossing. She mustered a tiny smile as I said, 'I do think you and Adrian are brave.' I had to say or do something.

That evening at home my mind kept straying to the plight of Jennifer and Adrian, alone with their newly widowed Dad. What if anything happened to me? If I was knocked down and killed? Worse – crippled, or blinded for life? All because I'd become a Lollipop Lady. What would happen to *my* two? The moneylenders would still want the exorbitant repayments, and Granville couldn't stay at home with them, not on an evening when he had to work as a waiter to earn extra. So many doubts flitted to and fro about the wisdom of being a Lollipop Lady. Was the risk worthwhile for less than £4 a week, even if it did keep the moneylender wolves a bit further away from the door?

Then I remembered that Christmas was coming, and there wouldn't be goose at all, let alone a fat one, if extra money didn't come from somewhere. Not that we'd *buy* a goose, but the rhyme 'Christmas is coming, the goose is getting fat' exerted me to action.

I made up my mind to try and be extra careful on the crossing and zealously watch out for those huge lumbering coal lorries and the nifty, crafty little cars that delighted in shooting out from behind them. Yes, I'd definitely stay on the job – God willing – till Christmas was over. And I did want to complete a year on the Lollipop job if possible, to experience every mood of the seasons in the Great Outdoors.

Life burst rapturously into a rainbow of delight next morning. All morbid thoughts flew out of the window (how do they, when it's closed?) as though they'd never assail me again. Five minutes before leaving home, adjusting my navy beret to withstand gale, hail, or snow, the letter box clicked open.

Caroline ran to see what it was. 'More demands and threats I suppose,' I muttered. But Caroline's voice held a new quality. A mixture of awe, dread, and anticipation. I began to tremble.

The telegram was to congratulate me on winning one of fifteen second prizes in a face cream competition! No matter that the first prize could have gone a long way in ridding us of the moneylenders – a thousand pounds – but I'd won a full-length suede or leather coat, to be made up in my measurements. Me, who hadn't had a new coat for years, let alone a posh new one. Caroline and I joined hands and danced round the bemused cat in jubilation.

Never before had I been a major prize-winner, and only twice before had I won a consolation prize – never a first, second, or third prize. We took *Competitor's Journal*, and I thought it well worth buying. It was going to be a lovely, lovely day, full of optimism, hope and joy. I couldn't wait to transmit my elation to all my friends at the crossing. Like a child, I wanted to tell everybody I was having a birthday. Well, not an actual birthday, being Aries, but that 'Whoopee!' kind of feeling. Marvellous! And being a Lollipop Lady had been the reason for my success. During a lull in crossings, I'd pondered the slogan to boost the brand of cream in the competition. Then it had come to me, like a bolt from the blue: 'As a Lollipop lady my skin needs –' followed by the name of the face cream.

My advice to anyone hooked on competitions, as in every other aspect of life, is if at first you don't succeed, try, try, try again. My experience proved also that it's useless thinking along the same well-worn lines. A slogan needs to be topical, up-to-the minute, novel – and sincere. That's where a new job, especially an out-of-the-ordinary one, can set one's mind thinking along fresh, original lines.

Alas, we only stay on Cloud Nine for a brief time. There's always the return to earth. After such a morning of rare happiness, my spirits sobered down during the duty, which finished at one thirty. Adrian had come down with a group of youngsters, obviously his Dad thinking it best that he didn't attend his mother's funeral. How relieved I was that Adrian was well out of sight down the snicket when I glanced up the lane to see if there were any more 'stragglers'. There were no children, but a slow procession was winding its solemn way down the lane: Adrian's mother's funeral procession.

As the plain oak coffin, massed with chrysanthemums of every hue passed by, I silently said 'Goodbye' and prayed that all her pain had now gone, and she was in Eternal Life. And that Adrian, Jennifer and their Dad would come to terms eventually with the crushing blow that fate had dealt them. Watching the gleaming black funeral cars crawling in dignified solemnity along the main road, slowing up other traffic, I pondered on the strangeness of life and, how much stranger, death.

Naturally, little Mrs Costa wasn't far away. She had been standing, mouth slightly ajar, hands coiled in the skirt of her floral pinafore, headscarf tied securely under her chin. But in respect to the dead, her curling pins had been removed, so there were no Dinkie rollers sticking out like miniature anti-aircraft guns at the ready over her forehead.

'Ee, Hazel,' she sighed, ambling up alongside me and hanging on to Lollipop, 'isn't it a shame? Ah was just saying to our 'Arry as ah were doing a bit o' ironing, it feels like Monday's Moist Misery, what wi' t'funeral an' all.'

When I looked perplexed, she grinned delightedly, shedding her pale mask of tragedy in the twinkling of an eye. 'You mean to tell me tha's nivver heard that saying, and bred and born in Yorkshire?' (Isn't it marvellous knowing something that nobody else does?)

After a bit more gossip, and the last few stragglers disappeared down the snicket, I took Lollipop to 'garage' her (I regarded Lollipop as a 'she'). I was sauntering across when there was a screech of brakes, and drawing to a flamboyant halt, in a brand new car, was Mrs Johnson, who lived near the end of the lane. Her eyes were sparkling. Nonchalantly, with what she hoped looked like practised ease, she got out and swung open the passenger door.

'Hop in, Hazel, I'll run you home – unless you're frightened! I've just passed my driving test, and dying to try myself out on somebody. It might as well be you.'

So the day, which had seen so many varied emotions for me, ended on a happy note, and I wondered how long it might be before I received my new leather coat – and how long before there'd be such excitement again.

Next morning I still had a slight 'hangover' of excitement after news of the competition win. Then I saw the navy and red of our postman's uniform as letters were pushed through the letterbox. I never suspected that lightning could strike twice – in a lucky kind of way. In the summer holidays Caroline had written a story about 'Micky, The Human Chimpanzee' for a competition in *Woman's Mirror*. Caroline's voice, even more excited than before, called out to me.

'Mummy, Mummy, come down, quickly!'

Flinging a flannelette sheet on the bed, I tucked the sides under. 'What's happened now?' I shouted down.

'It's a letter from *Woman's Mirror* – I've won first prize in the over-nine section of that children's story contest. You know, last summer...'

I ran downstairs and grabbed the letter. Surely I wasn't beginning to have hallucinations as I neared the dreaded age of forty? There, in the envelope, was £25-worth of premium bonds.

We joined hands, and Prince nipped out of the way. If at all possible, the dance of joy we performed was even wilder and more ecstatic than yesterday's gleeful frolic. I was beginning to feel that Santa Claus had a big sack somewhere loitering behind the back door, and he was letting wonderful surprises out day by day. It might go on for ever – could such pure, undiluted delight as we were experiencing ever be felt by a rich person? I doubt it. At that moment, Caroline and I were the happiest people in the world.

But life goes on. The bubble of happiness burst at lunchtime, and changed to boiling rage when Caroline, close to tears, emerged from the snicket on her way up for lunch (or dinner as we Northerners call the midday meal).

'What's the matter?' I asked, sniffing the air, which had suddenly turned foul.

'Jonathon has been rubbing dog dirt on my socks,' she answered, following up the remark quickly with 'Don't say anything, Mummy' – knowing my propensity for direct action when either she or Elizabeth were in any way threatened.

How quickly my daughters could read my mind, interpreting my expressions so correctly! That young swine Jonathon had only the day before been hurling stones at her. This latest bit of dirty work would not go unheeded.

Caroline had a key and went up the lane before I did. With bated breath I waited, scrutinising every face appearing round the snicket, hurrying others across and back to the other side quickly so as not to miss the bully. Ah! There he was – scruffy socks concertinaed round his ankles, cheeky impudent face, smothered in freckles, ginger hair. I grabbed his arm.

'Don't ever you dare touch Caroline again,' I began. 'If you do, I'll give you the hiding you deserve.'

I'd never seen any child alter from a bully to a coward as fast in all my life.

'Oh, boys will be boys,' smirked one stupid mother, passing me with a smile for Jonathon.

'There are boys and boys,' I snapped, almost hating her as much as the bully. 'If some stupid parents don't teach them ordinary decent behaviour they can't blame those who take the job on themselves, before school bullying becomes youthful vandalism.'

Another pitying smirk from her. I felt like knocking her block off with the aid of Lollipop.

Like April showers followed by May flowers, the next encounter was a laugh. A timid little chap who'd been given a lift in a car the other morning, by a driver with a big dog in the passenger seat, tapped my shoulder.

"Ullo, love. Know that feller who gave me a lift the other day? Tha knows, 'im with a great hefty dog – my God, what a hell of a time I had trying to get out. I was in t'seat and every time I made to open t'door, damned thing growled and bared his teeth. We were all three squashed together, it only being a short way to go. Even put his paw on me to stop me reaching for the door. Whew – and me pal thought it a huge joke. Couldn't stop laughing. I was later for work than if I'd waited for t'bus by t'time I managed to get out.'

'You'd better think twice in future,' I laughed, 'before allowing yourself to be picked up by strange dogs.'

Elderly Mrs Jackson from the old people's bungalows hobbled up next, walking stick tapping the pavement on every measured tread. I prepared to listen to her troubles.

'Ay lass, there's some rotten stuff in t'shops these days. Fancy, ah bought two vests last week, now after one has been washed, it won't even cover me sit-upon.' The old lady turned up her frayed coat collar against the biting wind, and waited for my response to such dastardly events.

'Never mind, Mrs Jackson, they'll make smashing dusters.'

It was 25 November already – only a month to go, then Christmas. Elizabeth and Caroline counted their savings, then went present-buying. I looked forward to seeing what they'd buy without me supervising them.

Caroline returned about four, sparkling-eyed and rosy-cheeked, darting quickly up to her bedroom to gloat over her loot before Elizabeth burst in with her parcels.

'Can I look?' I asked Caroline.

'These cost me 8s 11d,' she said, showing scarlet stretch slipperettes, trimmed with huge white fluffy pom-poms. 'D'you think Elizabeth will like them?'

I wondered how much Elizabeth's parting shot had had on her choice of gift: 'Remember, Caroline, I'm spending nearly 10 shillings on you!'

I came downstairs leaving Caroline eagerly cutting seasonable wrapping paper. There'd be Sellotape sticking everything together, besides the gift, before she'd finished.

During November it was almost dark before I finished the last crossing at half past four. There was snow in the wind on the 28th, but at midday we enjoyed a clear sunny hour or two.

Caroline was in the Junior Choir, and had to stay late after school on Mondays for rehearsal. It made me feel quite sick standing there in the gathering darkness, when all the others had gone home, thinking about her negotiating that narrow dark snicket by herself. It was a very different short cut in those dark autumn evenings from a bright bustling summer day.

I wished my eyes were searchlights to pierce the gloom as the minutes ticked away. Four twenty, twenty-five, half past four. Twenty to five. It would have been pitch black if it weren't for the street lights along the main road and the winking orange Belisha beacons at 'my' crossing. In daydreaming moments I pretended I was a star on Broadway, the Belisha beacons my neon lights, flickering out my name. Not *Lullaby of Broadway*, but *Lollipop of Huddersfield* – or something.

But on Mondays I was only a worried mother, hoping against hope that Caroline would appear, with her bright smile, out of the snicket, hand outstretched to take my own. My mind worked overtime, feverishly, mentally saying, 'Caroline, Caroline, come on…,' then at last, with a great sigh of relief, there would be a murmur of voices, girlish laughter, and a trio of hooded, gabardine-clad figures would emerge from the gloom. There's no relief quite like that of a mother when her chicks come safely home!

19

'Roll on Christmas!'

Another Monday tea-time at the end of November, Caroline and I had been inside the house, cosy, safe and warm, already in our slippers, when Elizabeth, who then had two buses to go on to school, then again coming back, thudded wildly and impatiently at the back door.

'Let me in, let me in!' she shouted before I'd time to open it. She shot past me to the blazing fire, bits of hail dropping from her face. 'I forgot my gloves, my fingers are frozen,' she wailed.

Elizabeth was at that awkward pre-teenage time when wearing gloves wasn't the fashion. She usually carried them rather than wore them – or forgot them altogether. It caused many an argument, especially when one little girl I took across the road complained she hadn't any gloves. She pushed her cold hands into her coat pockets, recorder and music book beneath her arm tight against her body. What a contrary life! Those who have gloves won't wear them, those who haven't any wish they had a pair. I promised the little cold musician that I'd bring her some gloves next day.

I was glad not to be an office girl, dashing for a bus on slippery roads, trying to look alluring, rather than warm, in stiletto-heeled shoes. Most of the younger females obviously preferred a spell in hospital with a broken ankle to appearing in public wearing suitable footwear. Even the boots some wore had ridiculously high heels. I was thankful to be in my uniform of thick-soled wellington boots. No matter how treacherously icy the roads, I was as sure-footed as a goat wearing them. Some fools still wore thin nylons, too, while I was snug in thick ribbed tights beneath my navy trousers.

Whichever end of life one is at, childhood or old age, there are problems to contend with. Next I listened to a tale of woe from poor old Mrs Jackson. Tears rolled round her wizened cheeks as she unburdened herself to me. She was a widow.

'Ay, Lollipop. My Luther used to do all the shopping for me in awful weather like this,' she said, wiping tears from her eyes. 'He'd never have let me put a foot out of doors if it was bad. You do miss 'em when they've been good uns. After they've gone. Be thankful you've still got yours, lass.'

The cold soon became too intense for her to stay talking any longer. Hitching up her skirt and gripping her walking-stick tighter, she asked, 'See me across Hazel – do you mind?'

As we slowly crossed I asked, 'What do you do these long dark evenings, Mrs Jackson?'

The old lady fished a crumpled, already damp handkerchief from her coat pocket. 'Me? Evenings? I watch television – and cry.'

Safe on the opposite side she turned and waved her stick in the air in a brave gesture of farewell. Then her thin weak voice called, 'Thank you, love! Ay, ah've just remembered something.' She gasped and wheezed as the sharp air made her catch her breath. 'My Luther had a habit of playing with his pyjama buttons. So one day ah said to him, "Ah won't sew 'em on again if you pull another off, you devil!"' She doubled up with laughter at the memory. 'So the Home Help asked for a needle and cotton. He'd pulled another one off. I think he must have gone a bit bonkers in his old age. Never time to do all there is to do when you've a job, then spending your time yanking buttons off yer pyjamas...'

The laughter stopped almost as soon as it had begun, her pale blue eyes awash with tears again.

'But ah loved every hair of his head,' she whispered, as snowflakes began to swirl softly round her, coming to rest on the old brown knitted 'shopping cap' and melting into the wool. That cap was only removed from her head on rare occasions – if the temperature soared into the seventies, or on Sundays. But the slim gold locket and chain that her Luther had bought for her one summer at Blackpool many years ago, when she was a young bride, stayed round her neck all the time. In the locket was a miniature photograph of Luther as a small boy, posing proudly in huge white sailor hat and suit.

November went out in a Thunder and Lightning Polka, with lashings of snow and rain to add to the pandemonium. The wind contributed to the end-of-year mayhem, too. Then, like a crock of gold at the end of the rainbow, shone forth a solitary gleam of pale yellow sunshine. I almost fell on my knees and worshipped it. All bad things, like the good, come to an end – in time.

All the elements weren't confined to the heavens that morning, however. Idly, I wondered why the men in an oncoming car appeared to be taking an undue interest in me as I stood, Lollipop at the ready, waiting for another lot of children. The car pulled up alongside me, and the chap in the passenger seat rolled down the car window. I went up to it and, putting on my 'Can I help you?' smile, I waited.

'Are yer ready for it, Lollipop? he grinned.

Before I'd time to reply, 'What?', swoosh! He squeezed a detergent bottle in my face. It oozed dirty soapy water and I couldn't do anything about it. Laughing like maniacs, they sped on their way.

A kindly middle-aged woman who'd seen the incident was even more indignant than I was.

'The rotten devils! You should report 'em, love,' she scowled, taking off her woolly scarf and wiping my face tenderly. I backed away as the mass of pink mohair was more of a threat than the water, bits of it going into my eyes. I realised how vulnerable I was, standing there. Like a clown in a fairground, I ought to open my mouth and charge a penny a time.

I soon saw the funny side, though, left by myself again. The picture I had of myself, like a latter-day Charlie Chaplin being assaulted with washing-up liquid squirted into my face, kept the corners of my mouth sliding up into a smile every so often. I wondered if they'd have dared do it to a policeman, though – I don't think so.

After that experience of being target practice, I felt even more abhorrence for those who enjoy shooting at those ducks that sail slowly past on fairground stalls. Inanimate targets they may be, but still I feel that somehow it's wrong to shoot anything that can't defend itself. I pondered the desirability of arming myself with a row of full water pistols for future crossing sessions...

I don't think those aggressive young men would have dared to shoot at John the gardener either. He came stalking homeward about four, hands as usual deep in his donkey jacket pockets, boots as thickly soled as an old family bible, flat cap fitting snugly on his head, to thwart any sneak wind that might try and lift it.

'Tha's got a mucky face, Lollipop,' he observed. 'Ain't yer washed it today?'

I told him what had happened.

'Rotten cowards,' was his verdict.

In winter John was more ruddier-cheeked and pot-bellied – because of the extra waistcoats – than in summer. But even hectic weather like that day's failed to ruffle his placid temperament. 'Ah take life, an' t'weather, as it comes. If we get good patches today, we'll have bad uns tomorrer.' He rubbed my cheek, in an effort to remove the streaks. 'Ne'er mind, Lollipop, variety's the spice of life.'

Off he clomped into Nellie's for his home-time packet of fags, then re-appeared, eyes twinkling merrily at some quip made to Nellie.

A swarm of birds flew over, all in the same direction – migrating to warmer climes, maybe. How I wished I knew how *they* knew, in their tiny bird brains, that this was what they must do? And if they, small as they were, had so much intelligence, why should anyone feel angry if someone called us bird-brained? Really, it's quite a compliment. I'd never get anywhere without signposts along the way, or a bus driver to take me where I wanted to be.

Still day-dreaming, I wondered more about those birds. How would they look with snow boots on, flying through the skies until they reached those fairer climes, when they could shake them off? How we humans spend too much money on briefly worn summer dresses and open-toed sandals, yet feel it's outrageous to spend a few more pounds on serviceable boots that would keep us happy, warm *and* upright for many winters without going out of date! Then, instead of dreading winter, we could draw the curtains open and gasp with delight at the winter wonderland before our eyes, and hurry to pull on boots and hooded coats to dash out and enjoy it. Life could be so much easier if we learned to accept and cope with Nature, instead of shivering and moaning in thin stockings and fine-weather shoes... Adapt to the seasons, and life becomes a song, not, as so often happens, a dirge.

December hurtled in more like white shots from cannons than a song. On the first crossing hailstones banged my face so ferociously that it stung. How I wished that somebody manufactured weatherproof face masks for Lollipop people in pretty colours, pink or apricot – with a couple of central red blobs for the cheeks and just the eyes showing, a bit like a yashmak.

The rest of the day had nothing to commend it, even when the cannons had stopped firing and peace was declared. Then we had torrential rain and gale-force wind, *and* it was Thursday, the morning when I had to go on the bus into town to pay bills. There was nearly £22 to pay for half-yearly rates – a big amount when moneylenders are breathing heavily down your neck, £15 to finish paying for a carpet, and other bills to pay.

Wet through and cold long before a quarter to nine, I wanted the morning to be over as quickly as possible. How I wished I could dash up home for a coffee and a Blue Riband biscuit in front of the fire – but I didn't get back till half past eleven, not having had a warm drink since seven thirty. Then there was barely time to rub my hair with a towel, change sopping-wet gloves, put the shopping and receipts for the bills in the Welsh dresser drawer, then run down the lane again to begin the midday session. Prince, lucky cat, rubbed against me and sympathised, then sprang back on to an armchair in front of the fire.

I was beginning to look forward to breaking up for the Christmas holiday as much as the children. When you go out to work it really feels to be holiday, even though housework has still to be done.

'Oh, roll on Christmas!' I said to John as I went to put Lollipop down the snicket.

'Roll on,' echoed the gardener, winking broadly. I must have looked a sight – hair hanging wet through against my cold face, which felt like marble when touched. My hair could not have been wetter if I'd washed it right there on the roadside. Hailstones had found their way into my wellingtons, making my feet squashy and soaked.

Cars, lorries, coal wagons, buses, all splashed and zoomed past as I stood in the centre of the road by the bollards. Whichever way I turned I was in no better position. The wind became so wild that the 'STOP – CHILDREN' sign was an absolute hindrance and menace to those within striking distance. Lucky police – when they were substitutes for a Lollipop Man or Lady they didn't have to use the Lollipop. Crossing patrols should not be compelled to either, on squally days when it's as much as anyone can mange to stay upright without the encumbrance of holding something like that. Holding on to tearful children's hands, watching the flow of traffic – and the wayward Lollipop – was physically and mentally exhausting. Though unseen, wind could be diabolical. I had one hand keeping my beret in place, the other controlling the lollipop, while bad-tempered motorists honked their horns as they fretted to get home, maybe for pre-Christmas parties.

Housework seemed never-ending on winter evenings, when I'd have loved to have cuddled up in front of the fire with a book: hot-water bottles to fill – and frequently to refill if the children were still awake when they went cold – ironing, baking, playing with Prince and her ping-pong ball… Granville was unable to take over, as he was out working most evenings to pay the moneylenders. What a shambles all work and no play made of our marriage!

However, I decided that a year working on the crossing would be enough. Next year, 1967, I'd make time for writing and occasionally doing what I wanted to do, and put my feet up – not have them swept from beneath me on that main road crossing. Next year I'd iron during the day, listen to a play – not have to stand ironing in the evening when I was dead tired to begin with, and having to move everyone out of the way for the ironing board, disrupting other activities.

Sorry as I would be to say goodbye to now familiar faces, sights and sounds, I wanted to leave while it was still a happy memory, and before I had – or caused – an accident, perhaps through being late one morning, or through sheer tiredness and nervous exhaustion.

Sometimes in bed I had nightmares. What if I didn't hear the alarm clock one of these dark winter mornings? What if I woke to the clock pointing to nine – how much carnage would have had happened down there on the road because I wasn't there?

Parents would blame me for the rest of my life. No, I'd never be able to live with myself if I caused something like that, because I know how I'd feel myself if something happened to my children through negligence, through someone failing in their duty.

And yet what a wrench it would be when the time came to hand in my 'uniform', never to see the navy cap, white linen summer coat and heavy white winter mac hanging behind the back door ready to be pulled on before racing down the lane. And the Large Men's knitted gloves, which weren't the slightest use in wet or extremely cold days. And my clompy wellington boots (it was a super excuse not to totter around in uncomfortable court shoes, working as a Lollipop Lady!).

This was the time, early December, when icicles hung from the walls, when children often came up sucking real frozen lollipops they had broken off trees and walls. I had many a real lollipop offered, but declined with thanks. It was hard enough trying to keep warm, without feeling frozen inside as well as out.

20

Bullies

Debbie was first down the lane. 'We're making paper chains at school today, Mrs Wheeler,' she told me gleefully. 'Lots and lots of different coloured sticky papers to loop into long chains. Green, red, purple, blue and yellow. I like doing that a lot better than arithmetic, don't you?' I fully agreed.

'Do you make your own Christmas cards as well, Debbie? It saves money and they're lots more fun than bought ones.'

We couldn't really afford to waste money on buying cards that year. Yet people always think there's something not quite right about making – or receiving – home-made ones. But anyone can pay for cards – if they have the money. Finding time to make individual ones is surely a better way of showing friendship?

I used to go to Art School, and there were sketch pads lying around at home. I'd have a go at making my own. It would be a complete relaxation, and save much-needed cash. So one evening, after tea, I set to work. I had a lovely time drawing and painting robins, Christmas trees, Victorian gentlemen and ladies, in tall silk hats and crinoline gowns, staggering under piles of parcels. But deep down, no matter how individual and personal each card was, perhaps I'd feel too ashamed to send any, and they'd get pushed into a drawer...

Elizabeth and Caroline, and the children I escorted across the road, were becoming more and more excited as the days drew nearer to breaking up. I often think that the anticipation is better than the arrival. Beverley and Brown Grandad had an extra glow about them as they waited on the pavement with me one morning, as though sparklers had been lit in their eyes.

'Miss...,' Beverley said, pulling at my coat (did some of them think of me as a kind of outdoor teacher?) 'Miss, one Christmas Eve I heard footsteps coming upstairs when I was in bed...'

Brown Grandad shook his head. Beverley still believed in Father

Christmas, and I wouldn't have been surprised if he didn't, too. Beverley continued her story.

'Then I heard the lavatory chain being pulled, and I knew it couldn't be Santa Claus, because he doesn't have to go, does he?'

Brown Grandad roared with laughter. 'Well, I suppose even he might get "tekken short" sometime, don't you think so, Lollipop?'

Monday 5 December was an especially hazardous morning. Frost and black ice made road conditions treacherous, and coming down the lane there only seemed to be me, in my wide duck-billed-type wellingtons, who was managing to remain upright. Everybody else had either been down on their backside or were trying to get back up. It was fun, as long as nobody hurt themselves. Some cars, slowly inching down the lane, found it difficult to stop when they reached the corner on to the main road.

I'd arrived intact, had been for Lollipop, and had crossed back to my position when a lorry lurched into the back of a stationary car yards from where I stood. The lorry driver, ready to blame the hesitant motorist, glared like a maniac, but quickly smiled sweetly when he realised the motorist was a young woman, blonde and shapely beneath her fur coat. Life's not fair to many!

Then George, the postman, who was still in hot pursuit of me, arrived just in time for an extra job. Another car had wedged itself into the back of the one in front as they turned the corner of the lane. Seizing the opportunity to show off his virility, George sprang to the rescue. Again, there was a female motorist in the first car.

'I'll see yer right,' said the hero of the moment, plonking the empty post sack on the icy wet pavement. Winking at me, he went to the lady's assistance. Out sprang the driver of the car behind, and there followed much good-humoured banter and laughter as they attempted to disentangle the two cars. Meanwhile, the young damsel in distress in the first car, warm and dry without so much as putting a leg outside to ease the situation, lit a cigarette, obviously used to male attention. In this life all you need to get attention is good looks, no matter what personality lurks beneath the exotic exterior. If life was a game of Monopoly, the good lookers would always end up on Park Lane, the mongrels among us in prison.

Bad weather brought out the best and the worst in people – some who passed by on the other side, others who went out of their way to help. One of the school dinner ladies was in a foul mood.

'Ah'm exasperated,' she announced, thumping Lollipop. 'When I do a job I like to be appreciated. But those foreign kids with funny religions, can't eat this, can't eat that, get my goat. My God, we send all that money to Oxfam to feed hungry children there, don't we – then us dinner ladies go to all the bother of cooking and dishing up decent meat and fish – and what do we get for our trouble?'

She gesticulated wildly, screwing her wizened face into ever more wrinkled contortions, imitating the hesitant speech of 'them ruddy foreigners'. I arranged my features into a sympathetic look.

'No meat, missus. Me don't eat meat. No eat fish. No fish. Have cabbage.'

Brown Grandad had come back up the snicket and joined in. 'There'd be enough and to spare in this world if they all used their noddles,' he said, tapping his head. 'Why the hell do the authorities insist on shoving food on to their plates they know damned well won't be eaten? 'Cos somebody or other decrees it. A lot of English youngsters don't like meat or fish either, but if they stay school dinners they have to take it.' Brown Grandad grinned. 'I'm saying nowt about your cooking, lass, but those school dinners – ugh!'

We spent a few more minutes putting the school system to rights, then Brown Grandad plodded off up the lane. I felt sorry for the dinner lady, though. Most don't go out to work for the money alone – they like to know that what they do is appreciated. Dinner ladies must feel so frustrated knowing their cooking largely ends up in the pig bins.

What a treat Tuesday was that first week in December! We enjoyed sunshine, blue skies, and pleasant mild temperatures throughout the day. In between crossing duties I took advantage of the sudden unexpected warmth to clean the bedroom windows. Not having any heating upstairs, that was usually a job to be put off. So housework went along with a swing, and life, for the moment, was good.

I ought to have known it couldn't last. The atmosphere changed as I finished the last crossing of the day at four thirty. Teenagers from the Secondary Modern school were hurtling down the lane as I turned to go up it. Caroline had gone up before me as usual. Hooligans is the word for the majority of them.

Two hefty lads of about fourteen were thumping two pig-tailed girls mercilessly. As they were running and fighting past me too fast, I could only yell, 'Bullies!' at the retreating figures and hope that someone would stop the thugs. Then I had a shock on entering the house. Livid red fingermark weals ran across Caroline's face, and she had obviously been crying. Having seen her safely across the road not long before, I couldn't understand what had happened.

'Two of those girls from the Secondary Modern pushed me against the wall, Mummy, and started hitting me across the face.'

From the description they were the two I'd felt rather sorry for. One was a gypsy-looking type who always wore down-at-heel wellingtons even in summer, and an open, buttonless coat over a thin shabby dress, her hair uncombed, face grubby. Her companion was moon-faced, slack-lipped, with a permanent downward curl of derision. Their victim, Caroline, had frequently remarked how sorry she felt for that particular couple, especially the gypsy-looking one, who never had ordinary shoes to wear. But that didn't absolve her from the way they had bullied Caroline, and other innocent children, probably through jealousy, realising they were loved and cared for.

I'd rather have been hit myself. Rage bubbled inside me. 'How I wish I'd watched you go all the way home,' I repeated, gently caressing the poor red face. 'If I'd seen what was happening, I'd have thrown the blasted pole to the ground – or brought it to crack them with.'

As I looked more closely I noticed five finger marks on the other side of her face, and I burst into tears. Me, looking after other children while my own was being attacked. I paced the room like a caged tiger. I needed to do something about it, then – not wait until next day. I wanted someone else to see those disfiguring red weals – wanted to show someone else why I was going to knock all hell out of those two swines! How would I be able to concentrate on the crossing next day, how could I give my full attention to looking after other children, when Caroline was in more danger than them? The only solution I could see was that Caroline would have to wait with me in the cold until half past four, then we would walk up the lane together. All because of those vile beasts!

I daren't risk her having another encounter with those two. They might slash her with a penknife and disfigure her for life – my mind was racing. How I wished Granville was coming home, so he could complain to the headmaster of the Secondary Modern on the phone. I tend to get a frog in my throat (a change from down my wellingtons) when worked up over anything. I was sure I'd collapse in a gibbering heap in I heard his voice on the telephone.

However, after tea I had composed myself a little and looked up the number, wanting to strike when the iron was hot. A wishy-washy voice listened, and replied, to my tirade about his pupils.

'I'm afraid there's nothing at all I can do about it, Mrs Wheeler,' he droned. 'They are not my responsibility once they're out of school. You are not the only parent of children in the Junior School who has complained, but as I say, it is entirely out of my hands.'

I could hardly believe what he was saying. I remembered our headmistress at the Grammar School, how she demanded, and got, courtesy, good manners, and kindly behaviour from every girl, all five hundred of them, in her school. If one was seen, or heard about, doing any misdemeanour, not giving up her seat to an adult on a bus, walking up to school past the boys' college, not wearing a hat, we were in detention for half an hour after school. It was as essential a part of our curriculum to be taught and apply correct behaviour as it was to pass exams. Indeed, our school motto was 'Honour Before Honours', and I had always tried to adhere to it. At first it had seemed strange to stand up when a mistress came into the room, then it felt strange not to. One girl, who had been in the same form as me, was so ingrained with that kind of courtesy that she continued standing up for anyone the rest of her life – even her husband whenever he entered the room!

Of course it was up to the headmaster what his pupils did outside the school! As with the teacher I stood my ground with about the swimming, once in confrontation I was like the old song, 'She fought like a tiger for her honour' – from being a timid, insignificant Lollipop Lady, I'd have taken on King Kong, Hitler, anyone, if I knew I was in the right!

'I entirely disagree with you,' I snapped. 'This isn't the end of the matter,' and replaced the receiver.

He may have fobbed off other parents in that manner, but he certainly hadn't heard the last of me. Thinking that because it was against the rules to cane pupils any more and his hands, so to speak, were tied, was ridiculous. If his were, mine most definitely weren't.

That evening I pondered all sorts of possibilities to safeguard Caroline, although she bravely kept saying, 'I'm all right, Mummy, don't worry.'

Should I telephone Mr Fiddes there and then, tell him to stick the job and the pole too? My emotions were in complete turmoil – I didn't know what to do for the best. God knows we needed the money, but I needed to know that Caroline was safe even more. But why should our lives be jeopardised by these rough elements? Why *should* they get away with everything spoiling life for others?

The following day I decided to sound out other parents' experiences with louts from the Secondary Modern. Not that all were badly behaved – it's always a minority that give a bad name to an organisation.

How I wished there were two of me – one working on the crossing, the other a private detective, forever tailing my daughter to ensure her safety! As I discussed the previous evening's happenings with some of the other mothers, a solution presented itself that hadn't occurred to me before. There was usually someone I knew going up the lane at the same time as Caroline. Why not ask if she could walk with them as far as our house?

Mrs Morrison was the first to offer, after relating what had happened to her, let alone a child.

'I know the girl you mean,' she exclaimed, as I described the gypsy-looking youngster with wellingtons and black straggly hair. Mrs Morrison was one of those young women who looked even more attractive wearing spectacles, because they were fancy ones, and green-rimmed, giving an aura of allure. Her green eyes opened wide with the drama of it.

'Guess what she did to *me* the other day! She had a long stick she'd obviously pulled from a tree coming through the wood from school, and rammed it up my backside! Cheeky little devil! She won't get a chance again though, don't you worry,' she said, the gleam of battle in her eyes.

'If she'll attack adults, what won't she attack?' I wondered. We had to laugh, though. I had a vivid mental picture of elegant Mrs Morrison, blithely homeward-bound with her dainty box of cream cakes for tea, being thus rudely accosted by Miss Raggetty Wellington Boots.

'Bet you thought it was one of your admirers giving you a playful poke in the rear, didn't you?' I teased.

Mrs Morrison giggled. 'Well, yes, I must admit, I did at first. But surely they wouldn't have pushed with such a vengeance!'

So that afternoon ended all right, with Caroline hand-in-hand with her going home. But all my fears came rushing back when I talked to another mother next day.

'What do you think that terrible monster – that girl – did to our Sarah?' related Mrs Taylor. 'Sarah and her pal were taking a short cut down the fields, then that flaming Wellington Boots and her crony grabbed our Sarah and Jane. You'll never guess what they did to them…!'

'No, what?' I breathed, my heart bumping in anxiety.

'Forced them on to their knees on the frozen grass, made them shut their eyes, pull their knickers down – and recite the Lord's Prayer all the way through. With their eyes shut!'

I had hardly recovered my composure after hearing about that macabre incident when another mother joined it.

'Well, what about our Robert – some of those hooligans from up yonder slashed his face with a knife once.'

By that time I was keyed up to the hilt, and craned my neck to see if I could catch sight of Caroline emerging from the snicket. But I knew I couldn't continue like this, relying on a passer-by to take her up the lane every day. My mind was made up. If nobody else dared to do anything about it, then the Lollipop Lady would.

21

'There's allus summat afore Christmas for somebody...'

*T*here was just time between the one thirty finish on the crossing and getting there again for three thirty for me to dash up the fields and encounter the headmaster of the Secondary Modern school face to face. But it was a damned nuisance. I had lots of jobs that needed doing and I enjoyed a bit of relaxation during that couple of hours. Nevertheless, someone had to act. They couldn't be allowed to get away with such behaviour, which might even end up in a real tragedy after what I'd heard from others.

The headmaster was pleasant enough, but secretly I considered him a complete wash-out.

'Oh yes, I do agree, we have one group who are really vicious,' he smiled, twiddling his pen, 'but there we are. What can we do?'

'That's what I'm asking you,' I smiled, though inwardly snarling. 'How about informing the police for a start?'

He spread out the palms of his hands in a gesture of despair. 'They already know. In fact, one policeman was appalled and shocked when he went into the home of the girl you complain about. The family live in a particularly rough slum area – father won't work, mother goes out cleaning – apparently don't bother about the children at all.'

'I'm very sorry for them, but I can't have my daughter intimidated every day, and when I'm working on the crossing I can't see her safely home myself. Something will have to be done before a tragedy happens. Bullying children smaller than they are can't be allowed to continue.' I could have added the incident with Mrs Morrison getting a poke up the rear end, but on second thoughts he might think I wasn't being sufficiently serious about the matter...

'Well, all I can do is speak to them and warn them they are in for trouble if they don't behave,' he finished lamely.

'In the meantime, how do we protect our children?' I wanted to know.

'I'm afraid I can't say,' was his feeble reply.

I was exasperated and, for once, lost for words.

'Hmm – Miss Hill, our headmistress, would have known how to deal with the situation,' I fumed, and stalked out of the room.

So that was that. I hurried down the fields shivering with both physical cold and apprehension. At one time, bullies would have been birched, perhaps given the 'cat o' nine tails'. Now, nobody seemed prepared to do anything apart from talk to them. Fat lot of good that was. In the meantime, any one of the Junior School children who happened to be going home when the Secondary Modern gang were at loose, were in peril. What a ridiculous state of affairs.

Near the top of the lane was a small private school. Those children were safe. Cars lined up outside to transport them, in their smart brown blazers, hats and school caps, to and from school. Those parents didn't have the worries that we without cars had. I used to think some of those children were too mollycoddled, but how I wished that my two were in such a privileged position, not to encounter bullies.

All I could do was impress on all the children on 'my' crossing never to walk alone, to keep in groups, and whenever possible to walk with an adult (that they knew). And after Mrs Morrison's stick incident, even they might not be immune from that gang's attentions!

I had been quite surprised to hear the headmaster's views that girls were frequently worse bullies than boys. But that fact was verified by Mrs Sanders, who went to the Workshop for the Blind every day.

'I can believe it,' she nodded sadly as I helped her across to the bus stop. We weren't supposed to help any but schoolchildren, but I couldn't stand aside when a blind old lady was relying on the good nature of motorists, and her white stick. 'Only yesterday I was jostled by a band of ruffians – sounded like girls – pushing me and making fun of my blindness. One pinched my stick for a few minutes, to see what I'd do – not very nice, is it?'

Oh, if only Guardian Angels were around when such dastardly happenings went on! We are all supposed to have one, but I think they are asleep a lot of the time.

How illuminating it was to listen to working wives discussing their lives. And how incongruous some could be. A group shuffled past me, puffing cigarettes, staggering with cases full of washing that they were trailing to the laundrette. No, they couldn't do without the 'extras' that going out to work provided. Yet the whole idiocy of some full-time working wives was summed up by one:

'Ay lass, yer don't have to bother about a bit o' muck. My house is just like Dirty Dick's. But I only go out to work so ah can pay for us fags and beer money.'

Her friend explained her reasons for going to work. 'I don't like leaving t'kids, but we couldn't afford to keep car if I didn't go out.'

Priorities had all gone haywire. Surely husbands preferred a clean, cosy home to an abode like 'Dirty Dick's' to come home to, instead of their wives smoking themselves to a cancerous end and living in a dust-laden place – and what was wrong with a walk instead of riding everywhere in a car, and the added worry of hire purchase?

Next morning, the eleven-plus exam was 'Verbal Reasoning'. Oh, if only those working mothers with 'Dirty Dick' houses had a few lessons in a reasonable way of living!

The beginning of December was sunny, then stormy, swiftly changing to beautiful blue skies, then grey, gusty wind and rain, followed by hailstones. Who could ever be bored with the English weather?

On the 8th, back on the crossing at one, the sight of an ambulance flashing its blue lights outside the newsagents further down the road interested passers-by so much that they let the buses they intended to catch go without them. Instead they stood craning their necks, doing their utmost to 'see summat'.

I must admit, I was curious too. After a few minutes' tension, everyone holding their breath and not daring to cough in case they missed anything, the ambulance men appeared carrying a stretcher, and on it a lifeless figure wrapped in a deep blue blanket. I saw that the face was covered too – obviously whoever it was had died. The ambulance sped away, and the little knot of onlookers buzzed into a babble of speculation.

'What's up – somebody been murdered or what?' queried John the gardener, blowing pipe smoke into the air.

'Was it an accident?' George wanted to know, rounding the corner after the second postal delivery of the day. 'Come to t'pictures with me tonight, Hazel?' he added hopefully.

We didn't have long to wait to find out what had happened. That bearer of tidings, good, bad, and indifferent, Mrs Costa, bustled up armed with the facts before it was time for me to go home. She had left the door of her smoke-blackened cottage open in her hurry to impart what she had seen. A wicker basket, on the pretext of going shopping, was on her arm.

'Ee, Hazel, what do you think to that?' she said, grabbing Lollipop for support after the excitement.

'What's happened?' We were eager to know as much as she was to tell.

'There's allus summat afore Christmas for somebody...' Mrs Costa revelled in retaining her superior knowledge for as long as possible. Suspense was the thing. 'Poor sods. Going to Bridlington too tomorrow, to retire. Got a bungalow. Sold their terrace here, and then this happens. Doesn't do to plan ahead at all, Hazel. It just doesn't do.'

I glanced at my watch. Time was flying. If she didn't get a move on it would be time for coming back down again.

'Tell me, then – what happened – who was it?'

Mrs Costa shook her head dolefully, adjusting her curling pins beneath her headscarf, reluctant to curtail the drama that only she could impart. She put the basket on the pavement, and wiped a tear away. Her mouth, unadorned with lipstick, trembled.

'They're all dying off in our row. Like ten green bottles. One after t'other. Oh yes, well, as I was saying – it was Mrs Cartwright. Did you know her? Three doors up from us. I was speaking to her less than an hour ago. I can't believe it...'

'Yes, well, I shall have to be going in a minute...'

'Hang on, hang on, if you want to know – she said she was just popping across to t'shop for one or two things. Off she went. Next ah knew, ambulance men were outside t'shop. She'd sailed in, large as life kinda thing, asked for what she wanted – he's new, that young lad behind t'counter, y'know. Nobbut fifteen or sixteen. What a shock for him! Anyhow, Annie had asked him for t'stuff – then simply slumped down dead in front of him! White as a sheet – he ran across and banged t'door for Annie's husband. Oh my God, what a state he's in. Ah'd best get back and see how he's going on. So long, Hazel. Watch yer step.'

Off she trotted, with the empty wicker basket, muttering darkly to anybody who might hear her, 'In the midst of life we are in death...'

That took my mind off Wellington Boots and her gang for a while. But when I was coming back from the crossing at half past four there she was, with her fat, moon-faced friend. This was my opportunity.

'Hey, you two,' I said, standing in front of them, 'if you ever touch my daughter, or any other child who is doing you no harm, I'll do the same to you. And worse. *And* I mean it. Do you understand?'

In answer I received a mouthful of obscene abuse.

I was trembling as I turned the key in the door. Snow was blowing in the wind and rain. Caroline and the others who had been attacked must have been terrified out of their wits – those girls looked the picture of evil. Looking into their eyes was like gazing at Satan himself.

It was Friday already, with a violent wind gusting round the crossing corner. One small boy was overcome by it and fell, covering his bare hands and knees, which were red with cold, with slimy black mud. His gabardine was streaked with mud as well.

'Up you get, love.' I lent a helping hand, propping Lollipop against the wall. 'Good job I carry plenty of tissues. Let me see, no blood, only mud.'

I jollied him up and wiped the muddy parts dry. 'Thank you,' he smiled shyly, waving as I left him safely on the opposite side.

Little incidents like that made my job infinitely worthwhile, despite the non-princely wage at the end of it all.

I was not as successful with the next child who slipped and went down. He refused to get up until his mother came back from Nellie's shop. When she did, and saw him in a tantrum and in the mud, she gave him a sharp slap on his behind, which jerked him smartly back into a vertical position.

'Barry's troubled with dermatitis,' she confided. 'He's a nervous little lad, so I daren't be too hard on him.'

Gardener John was sauntering by. 'Have you ever tried Epsom salts, lady?' he asked the already flustered mum.

Her face flushed, and she stammered, 'Epsom salts, Epsom salts?'

'Yes. It might sound daft, but when ah was a lad and suffered with it, dermatitis, I had to mix Epsom salts with a drop o' watter. Rubbed it into the affected parts, and ah've never had it since.'

I don't know if John's remedy was tried, but on the crossing one heard the strangest things. Nevertheless, some of the simple cures often prove the best.

The wind was howling in wintry rage in the tea-time darkness as I waited for children to arrive at the crossing on the opposite side. Yet even such atrocious weather did not deter the lonely from seeking out an available human being, to hear a mortal voice above the roar of the wind, before the night closes round them, shutting out the rest of the world till next day.

Old Mrs Jackson was one of the lonely. Frail as she was, with her home a quarter of a mile or so up the main road, it must have taken her ten times as long to walk it as could a younger, stronger person. Yet she battled along to have a few words with me.

'Hello, Mrs Wheeler,' she panted, resting on her walking-stick in an effort to get her breath back. 'I thought I'd have a word with you before you go. It shortens these long winter nights – and there's no one else will hang about in weather like this.'

'Why not come up with me for a bit of tea then?' I offered.

'Thank you very much, love.' The wrinkled face smiled. 'Perhaps when the weather gets better. I'm so grateful for being asked, though. I might not be able to get back if the fog comes down as well.'

'Granville will see you home safely,' I said (depending on what time he gets back from the waiter job, I thought).

'Better not – ah've to learn to depend on meself now.'

'So what will you be doing tonight then?' I asked.

'Ay lass,' she moaned, voice hardly audible above the wind, which occasionally pushed her up against me so I had to put out a steadying hand, 'it's bad now it's getting on for Christmas. It's worst time o' year for old folk like me. The times I've started to write a few cards, then shoved 'em away again in a drawer. Ah just can't bring meself to put "Edith" and not write "Luther" as well when I sign them. It's me first Christmas without him, love, and oh, it *is* lonely.'

'I bet it is,' I sympathised. 'But will you help make *our* Christmas happier – we always have the same people, and it's a bit boring sometimes. We'd love you to come.'

Her eyes misted beneath her spectacles. She laid a hand on my arm.

'That's very kind of you, Mrs Wheeler – Hazel – but we used to have some friends who asked us every year. They'd be offended if I made other arrangements. But I haven't heard from them yet. And it's the ninth today, isn't it? So thank you all the same, but I wouldn't want to offend anybody.'

Like a wraith, she disappeared into the night.

Thick, dense fog was the enemy weatherwise on Monday. Nobody, not even Mrs Costa, could have said for certain, if she looked out of their lavatory window, whether it was man, woman or beast on the crossing. I simply merged into the greyness in my once white coat, except when traffic headlights pierced the gloom. I'd wound a thick scarf round my neck, and tried to stop myself breathing in the fog and traffic fumes. I didn't want acute bronchitis as a legacy of my year – almost – as a Lollipop Lady. I probably resembled Al Capone in that get-up, only my eyes showing, ready to leap forward with my guns and hold the next car to ransom.

Some hate winter, but there are plus factors. I adored the smell of Vick vapour rub, and the glow of a fire casting apricot-coloured shadows on the walls as we listened to a play on the radio – being able to get into a cosy dressing-gown not long after tea, something I daren't do in the height of summer.

It was just such a day of thick fog when Caroline and the others in the school choir were scheduled to go and sing at a school for immigrant children. A special bus was being laid on, and the school was some way out of town. As the time drew near when I knew they'd be leaving, I gave a silent prayer that the bus, on its errand of bringing joy, would not tip over into Aspley Canal on the way there or back. Everyone was saying the same old cliché: 'You can't see a hand in front of you'. My anxiety once again proved to be quite unnecessary. The bus didn't topple into the canal, and the carol-singers returned safe and sound.

Don't we add to life's miseries by imagining disasters that *could* happen, but ninety-nine times out of a hundred don't?

22

Home cooking

*T*he so-called unlucky 13th can often be a contradiction, and Tuesday 13 December was an absolute joy, especially in contrast to the previous day. It was clear, fine and marvellously sunny, I could see the hills in the distance, and everybody seemed to be smiling again. The wheels of life were turning smoothly once again in our little corner of the world, and God was in his heaven. The postman's wife down the lane, who was happily married (her husband hadn't the roving eye of the postman who kept asking me out), felt impelled to do something tangible to celebrate such a winter bonus as that glorious weather.

'Come on, Paul,' she greeted her fair-haired little boy as he emerged from the sunlit snicket, 'let's buy some cream cakes for tea!'

Paul, who had recently lost his front baby teeth, gave a gappy grin of delight, and hand in hand they went off in anticipatory glee.

There seemed to be more time to achieve things that lovely day. Or maybe it was just that there really *was* more time when you didn't have to change soaking wet outdoor clothes all day, and mop up muddy carpets and floors.

The sunshine was like an injection of energy. I polished furniture until it gleamed invitingly and positioned vases of twigs and holly on the Welsh dresser, transforming the room into a suitably old-fashioned, Victorian-looking delight. Why pay for bought decorations when so much better ones were freely available in the woods?

I'd even had time to prepare vegetables for a casserole, lots of root vegetables – turnip, carrot, onions, haricot beans, lentils – gorgeous! How I loved to come in from the cold and smell a meal cooking in the oven, pretending that somebody else had made it for me. There was just the HP sauce bottle to plonk on the table and chunks of bread – a meal fit for a king.

Then my mood of elation was brought to an abrupt halt. Back inside after the last, tea-time crossing, I swooped into the kitchen and banged into an open cupboard door that I'd forgotten to close when I'd rushed back to the crossing earlier. All happy thoughts of the casserole and a pleasant evening writing Christmas cards vanished in a sea of stars. Reeling, I staggered to look in the mirror, always more bothered about any permanent scar on my face and forehead than any physical hurt. A big red lump disfigured my forehead, completely altering my mood of sweetness and light to one of darkness and diabolical anger at having to try and do two jobs at once – especially being a Lollipop Lady, which entailed coming and going throughout the day, always racing against the clock.

Caroline and I couldn't tuck into the casserole when it was ready because Elizabeth hadn't returned from school. At half past five we wondered about telephoning the police. At a quarter to six there was a demanding thud at the back door.

'What's the matter with you?' Elizabeth demanded crossly, at the sight of my tear-blotched face. 'I *told* you there was a rehearsal for *Patience*.'

Her school was hoping to present the Gilbert and Sullivan operetta in the spring. With rushing around trying to get through a thousand and one jobs at once, I'd either not heard or had forgotten. All thoughts of writing Christmas cards had gone. There's nothing like a resounding crack on the cranium and a dash of anxiety to sap the energy and drive from even the most tenacious Lollipop Lady – a Lollipop Lady who was adept at comforting others, both old and young, but one who, when faced with her own fears, made a terrific mountain out of them. Fortunately, the ugly mountain I'd foreseen developing on my forehead only remained a black and blue bruised hillock. But I kept peering in the mirror, and opened and slammed the offending cupboard door a number of times, swearing at it.

Next morning everything, including the crossing pole, was coated with penetrating white frost. Can you imagine what it is like to turn out of a warm cosy house, then encircle with your hands a pole of sub-zero temperature? Why doesn't someone invent a winter coat for Lollipop poles, and a proper garage for them in wintertime?

'I'm sure I'll end up with rheumatoid arthritis, gangrene or frostbite on my fingers,' I moaned to John the gardener. 'And what if I've to have them amputated – I'll never be able to write again…'

'Tha'll be reet,' smiled the gardener, reassuringly. Nevertheless, I tried not to touch Lollipop with my fingers once I had it across the road, and let it rest against my coat, but felt a bit daft.

When there was nobody to take across the road, I tried to stand the blasted thing against the wall, but it slid to the ground, as if in the throes of a heart attack. I kept looking at my watch, willing the hands to spin round to half past nine. People, I mused, ought to be able to do what animals do in winter, hibernate. Prince, our cat, was better off than me, even refusing to go outside to the 'toilet' and making a determined dive for her ashes tray instead. Not being able to afford real cat litter stuff, I filled an old blackened baking tray with soil for such eventualities. It had drawbacks. Sometimes, to my horror, an earthworm, pink and wriggling, was brought inside with the garden soil. (Miss the crossing time, or get rid of the worm...?)

On such atrocious mornings, when Prince used the tray, I had to take it outside to empty while she leapt lightly back on to her armchair and, through half-closed eyes, watched the stupid human – me – going out into the frozen wastes of winter.

'If that's being a person, not an animal, then you can stick it!' she seemed to purr contentedly, her face going deeper into smugness.

That morning many of the mothers had 'slept over' and came scurrying down the lane, nearly falling over, wiping dewdrops off scarlet-tipped noses, panting, anxious, full of guilt.

'Sorry Hazel, couldn't bear to get out of bed,' was an oft-repeated apology, as I was about to go off duty.

I felt especially sorry for the three little boys whose dad had left their mother and them for his exotic-looking secretary. I'd seen her without her make-up once – face hard and insensitive-looking, not a patch on the boys' mother. The youngest was red eyed and snivelling.

'Mummy's not feeling well. She didn't get up to make our breakfast, and we haven't had time to make any.'

'I'm hungry,' wailed his brother, while the eldest kept a miserable silence.

Once involved with problems of 'my clients' I soon forgot about the coldness of Lollipop, and nine thirty arrived sooner than I'd imagined. But what heaven to dash home and spread my hands in front of the fire before taking my coat off – then glorious hot coffee, with Prince lapping warm milk from the saucer.

Later, going to the crossing for midday, I noticed eighty-three-year-old Mr Mallinson, a one-time stable boy and groom, sawing through the trunk of a tree in a front garden.

'Oh, you're not cutting that lovely tree down are you?' I paused to ask.

'Aye, it's what they want,' he replied, jerking a thumb in the direction of the house. He wiped his nose on his shirt sleeves. "Appen it'll let a bit more light in, but ah've passed this tree ivery day of me life for t'past forty-odd years. Ah'll be sorry to see it go. It's like killing an old friend.'

I was shocked. I had always admired that tree too, watching the leaves change colour through the seasons. Now old Mr Mallinson was earning a few shillings to augment his old age pension by felling it, wielding the saw like someone half his age. He had no need for an overcoat when active work such as that was in progress. If only neighbours didn't move, allowing new people to alter the appearance of well-loved gardens!

'Well, if it's what they want,' he said. With check cap on his grey, thinning hair and threadbare muffler round his neck, old Mallinson knew the secret of good health. Part of his philosophy was not standing about, but keeping busy, preferably outdoors, not huddling over a fire.

How I hated seeing trees being cut down. I'd prefer our house to be surrounded by trees, to keep out prying eyes. Few value privacy these days, I thought – me, who stands on view to the Public at Large. The trend then was everything 'open plan' – glass doors, no fences or hedges. People seem to be afraid of solitude, being alone with their thoughts. Constantly the majority seemed to prefer being surrounded by people and noise – blaring 'pop' – ugh!

Elizabeth offered to bake Christmas cakes for me after school. Yes, they ought to have been made back in November, but I had had no money to buy ingredients. I gradually bought them bit by bit when I collected my wages: candied peel, mixed fruit, all the lovely things that combine to make such an essential part of pre-Christmas. And the smell of them baking, that delicious aroma permeating the whole house, even when we were in bed – far better than buying a ready-made cake.

There were only eleven more days to go before Christmas Day itself when the cakes came out of the oven. Mrs Beeton would not have approved, but Mrs Beeton's life ran on more organised lines than that of a Lollipop Lady.

Thursday was grey and drab, murky, uninteresting – not the type to inspire daydreams. Hard frost had more to commend it. However, it was Thursday, and pay day. I went to town on the nine thirty-five bus for a big buy-in, which never failed to brighten the dullest day. I spent right, left and centre, albeit only in shillings not millions. Sometimes it was an indulgence even to be able to afford food, after the regular money that had to be paid into court. Oh, how different Christmas could be if all those debts brought on by dealing with moneylenders weren't a constant scourge!

Before becoming a Lollipop Lady, bringing in a few pounds, there had been days when all the housekeeping money had gone on paying off those interminable bills. On such days I had desperately searched cupboards for hidden tins of beans, made scones from flour skulking at the bottom of the bag, and worried myself silly what to give the cat.

Poor old John had an accident that Thursday – his left eye was extremely bloodshot and watery.

'A bough from one of the trees in the grounds of the old people's bungalows swiped it,' he explained wryly. 'Ah'd bin chopping dead wood down and making sure they all had plenty of firewood for Christmas.' He put a hand over the eye. 'Don't I look a bugger?' he laughed.

'No you don't,' I replied warmly, recalling my own worries after bumping into the cupboard door. 'You always look like an Adonis to me and you're so kind to all of them. You're wonderful, black eye and all!'

'Good old Lollipop,' he laughed, hugging me, 'tha's made my day.'

At about a quarter past four young Miss Ritchie, an Infant School teacher, came up to me, a worried expression creasing her brow.

'Mrs Wheeler, have you seen two small boys playing about? They left school at half past three, and only live at Mayfield Avenue. Their mothers have been down to school to see me, absolutely distraught – they still aren't home...'

By then it was almost dark, but I couldn't help, having seen no little boys loitering by the crossing at all. How I wished that mothers of children in the Infant classes would collect them from school – so much time and anxiety could be saved running around searching for them.

The scamps must have turned up, though, for I never heard anything more about them.

23

Anticipation

*C*aroline was busy making Christmas presents for her dolls and old
teddy bear those dark evenings. I helped her to stitch together a
green and white check gingham bikini top and panties for Mitzi.

'Don't you think she'd prefer a bit of cuddly warm fur?' I suggested. But
we hadn't any, so Mitzi would be in her new bikini on Christmas
morning.

The row of small shops in whose doorways I sheltered at the home-time
crossings were fun in the days before Christmas. Their electric fairy lights
flickered on about half past three, just when the Infant School children
came toddling out of the snicket.

'Oh, aren't the lights *luvly?*' they gasped in admiration. After they were
all safely on their homeward way I gazed at the contents of those brightly
lit windows for so long, waiting for the older children to emerge, that I
almost knew them by heart. Pacing backwards and forwards to keep
warm, I hoped I didn't look like the Guard at Buckingham Palace, or a
soldier on sentry duty in the war.

Supermarkets may have had all the cheap 'offers', but they could never
replace the intimacy and hotchpotch of toys, games, selection boxes and
compendiums that proudly took their place in the small independent
shops: gift boxes of talc, soaps, be-ribboned and with 'Christmas
Greetings' across the front, usually Lavender, Lily of the Valley, or
Magnolia – how to choose which one…? Then what indecision, wasting
time sniffing through the cellophane wrappings, who to give what? (Save
time by buying all the same – that's what I did!)

The advantage that those little shops had was that they willingly 'put on
one side' gifts for collection and payment nearer Christmas. This was
especially important when a mother wanted a particular doll or toy, but
couldn't afford to pay for it there and then. It was assured for Christmas Eve.

Nellie's little shop had a hand-written card in the window. 'Toys,
books, anything held till Christmas.' I smiled when I read it, picturing

poor Nellie, with all the ordered toys in her arms, unable to do anything else until they were claimed on Christmas Eve morning! What a joy to see the relief in a mother's eye, coming out of the shop having secured a few presents for her children's stockings, knowing also that they would not be discovered in the house before.

In between the infants and juniors crossing, I remembered an aunt telling me about her childhood. Long before the Welfare State, her father had died and her mother had had to take in washing and go out 'charring', cleaning for better-off ladies. There was no money for toys, so Annie, determined that her long black stocking would not be empty on Christmas morning, polished a tiny toy brass kettle she had been given the Christmas before until she could see her face in it. She wrapped it in brown paper, tied it with string and put it in her stocking to be opened on Christmas Eve, then went into the wood to gather firewood for her widowed mother.

Even in the so-called affluent 'sixties, there were still some who, through various circumstances, couldn't find cash for the 'extras' – termed necessities by others. Even if some dads received a cash bonus or gift before finished work on Christmas Eve, it would come too late to be sure of buying whatever had been hoped for.

Nellie was so understanding. 'If they can't pay me before Christmas I don't mind waiting till after. I don't want any kiddie to be disappointed if I can help it.'

What a worthwhile service her small shop gave, even at some inconvenience to herself. Often she uttered an exasperated 'Damn!' if she snagged a nylon on the piled-up boxes behind the counter.

'Me back cupboards are absolutely stuffed with put-by goods,' she smiled good-naturedly – and the twinkle in her blue eyes showed that she loved it!

In the window of the paint and wallpaper shop were adorable wicker baskets. with rolls of wallpaper sticking out of them – all the rage among teenagers then. I ordered one for Elizabeth, and it was taken out of the window and kept for me to collect. 'Any time up to six o'clock on Christmas Eve,' the owner said.

Standing there, I was almost in tears, a big lump in my throat, picturing our eldest daughter finding the basket on Christmas morning, with lots of other gaily wrapped little presents inside.

From my Thursday wages I'd already bought pretty lace-edged underwear, pink, hand-made chocolates, and a teenage doll with a complete wardrobe. Those wouldn't be enough to fill a basket. I pulled myself together – where was the money going to come from to buy the Parker pen, theatre tickets and new boots that I longed to give her?

It was a sad day, the last one of the week. There in the cold, leaf-filled gutter, right where I stood, lay a half-grown cat, pale ginger and white, like underbaked gingerbread lined with snow, its pretty pale blue eyes glassily open to the grey December sky. No one attempted to remove it. There was no Samaritan on the Crossing for poor, main road Ginger. Many, curious, paused and peered, then passed by. One chap, to my disgust, kicked it with his boot toe.

'Just seeing if it's dead,' he muttered, as I gasped in horror.

I tried to avert my eyes, hoping that someone would take the poor corpse away. Then, when one of the older schoolboys ran at it and began kicking it like a football, I flew at him in a range.

'Don't you care about animals? Their dignity – even in death?' I screamed, close to tears. By that time I had been keeping a silent communion with the dead animal for almost an hour. In death, I felt to have established some rapport with Ginger. I was its Guardian for the final hours on earth. If only a kindly policeman would appear, so I could ask about Ginger's decent dignified removal.

In desperation, wanting to stop any more unfeeling kicks at the prone figure lying there at my feet, I went into Nellie's, making sure no children were approaching first.

She shook her head in sympathy. 'They shouldn't have 'em on a main road. But I can't pick her up with the same hands I'm serving with, Lollipop – dead cats and jelly babies don't go well together. But I'll tell somebody about it when you've gone. If I see anybody.'

'But I want something done before I leave the crossing,' I urged. 'I can't bear to think of it being slung into a dustbin or squashed under another car.'

I went back to my vigil over little main road Ginger, and said prayers for its soul, that he – or she – might be now in the heaven that is for both people and animals, and never again need fear to walk in peace, never again be mowed down by a speeding car, and left as though a cat doesn't matter. It does. Far more than its murderer.

A few minutes before it was time to go home, one of the boys who lived in a large house nearby came out with a large brown bag.

'I think it's our Sandy,' he said solemnly. 'Mum says she hasn't seen him for ages. I'll see to him, he'll be all right now,' the lad comforted me, seeing my tear-stained face. 'We loved him such a lot, he was happy.'

So Sandy, as I now knew he was called, was wrapped gently in the bag and taken home to the back garden for burial under an apple tree. 'Two others of our cats were killed here,' Kevin, as he said he was called, told me.

'Well, I do hope you won't risk any more cats' lives, Kevin – it isn't safe for them living near a main road.'

I said goodbye to Ginger, thankful that he had enjoyed kind owners in life, and that at the last I had watched over him, with love.

Anna, a Hungarian lady who lived a few doors further up our lane, was hurrying down as I went up home. She was in her usual frenzy of excitement, swinging a child's shoe in one hand, her latch key in the other.

'Diane has come home wearing only one shoe, and she's going to her Daddy's Works Party tomorrow. She hasn't another decent pair...'

Breathless but triumphant she caught me a minute or two later. 'Aren't boys awful?' she laughed with relief. 'The caretaker found her shoe in the boys' toilets. Luckily not down one.' She started to laugh, unable to stop for ages.

'If you'd seen her, Hazel, hopping on the freezing doorstep, with only one shoe on, after hopping on one leg all the way from school!'

Anne slapped me heartily on the back and tripped over the pavement edge into the gutter, still throwing her head back with laughter and swinging the shoe jubilantly up and down. It was a wonder I didn't get a slipped disc, all the hearty thumps my back had to take!

It's a good thing we can be so resilient. In the depths of despair one moment, flinging ourselves about in sheer merriment the next! The shoe incident proved how relative is the meaning of happiness to the individual. If a wealthy parent's child had a shoe hidden due to a schoolboy prank there would have been plenty more shoes at home – no urgency, no despair, no anxiety that her child may have to forego the happiness of a Christmas party because she had no shoes to go in.

I wondered if it was harder to make a rich woman happy – to make her roll about the road, consumed with an all-enveloping sense of relief and delight? Maybe poorer mortals do know true happiness more intimately, even if they are more acquainted with grief as well.

'Christmas is OK, but what a lot of work it means,' sighed Mrs Morrison. 'Everything to be spick and span, polished, decorated, besides the non-stop buying – whew!' Laden with carrier bags, she laughed with happiness as she passed. 'But I'm glad I have a family to make supper for,' she added.

Money as well, I secretly thought, having seen her so many times in the last few days with parcels galore.

Everyone was rushing about like ants as I stood on the crossing. What a lot I could be achieving if I was at home, instead of just standing there, waiting. I could almost read the minds of shoppers: hands on the door of one shop – a change of mind – try another, might be cheaper – scurrying here, racing there – dropping parcels in the middle of the road, bringing traffic to a screeching halt – generous, festive smiles of apology and acceptance as drivers waited until Grandma's new pink bloomers or Dad's Christmas socks and tie were retrieved from slush-covered roads. Dashing here, dashing there, bumping into one another, nearly poking eyes out with Christmas tree prickles. Loving it. Laughing, joking. 'All the best!' 'Same to you!' – even from one old enemy to another in those final days leading to Christmas. Adoring every harassing moment, though swearing, 'Ah'll be glad when it's all over...'

One of those on-the-go non-stop shoppers walked back with me up the lane. 'I don't know what on earth to do, Hazel. I've been varnishing our dining-room table. A surprise for me husband. Well, it certainly will be a surprise.' It was better than any TV 'soap' waiting to know the outcome of all the cliff-hangers I was told. 'Then I remembered some more stuff I'd to get. Forgot about our Rover who'd been lying peacefully on the rug all morning.' I was glad she lived further up than me, wanting to know the outcome. 'Well, you'll never guess what happened – yesterday it was. Postman had left a parcel, seeing I wasn't in. On't doorstep. "Greetings. Merry Christmas." All that palaver, tags all over it. I'll say Merry Christmas! He's usually been and gone before I go out. But he was late, it being Christmas. Our Rover can't stand postmen. He was in such a frenzy the bloody dog leapt on to me table. Paw patterns all over t'new varnish, and carpet too. As if there isn't enough to do without having to do all that again!'

'Well, your husband certainly will have a surprise,' I laughed.

'Anyhow, life 'ud be boring if it all went straight sailing wouldn't it? So long! Merry Christmas, Hazel.'

She *could* have locked the dog in another room I suppose. But you don't think, do you, until it's too late. And when we want to give somebody a treat, common sense frequently flies out of the window. She could have varnished it on a sunny morning in spring, leaving Rover in the garden – but there wouldn't have been the same breakneck thrill of having a brainwave and getting on with it there and then, trying to get everything done at once for the Biggest Festival of the Year.

But I have found that the more harum-scarum the person, the more fun they are. My friend certainly had given her table a brand new look, and when we look back, to Christmases Past, it's those very dilemmas that provide most laughs. How utterly boring are those families where nothing goes wrong!

I remembered the year when, as usual, we needed extra money, and I became a GPO Christmas casual. With the money I was thrilled to be able to buy 'big' presents, not just socks and handkerchiefs in gift boxes kind of thing. It was 1952, the year we were married. My stepfather was a card addict, and confined to the house much of the winter, with bronchitis, he played Patience for hours on a rickety, collapsing old table. I decided to buy a proper card table, and pictured his look of surprise at being presented with such a big present, unwrapping the parcel to disclose the smooth dark green felt and firm legs of the new card table.

Giving is so much better than receiving, especially when you can give what you know is really wanted. But then Mother had covered it with Formica to save the green felt! How furious I'd been!

It was time to write letters to Father Christmas – just for the fun of it, since deep down we all know who it is lurking behind the whiskers and red cloak. Elizabeth, notoriously bad at spelling, began her letter to Santa: 'Dear Farther Christmas...' Some might say how silly at twelve years old – but sillier to grow up too soon. Magic and fairy tales don't last for ever, and like me she preferred to hang on to whatever bit of make-believe there still was in Christmas, and, in thinking it to be, somehow making it so.

There wasn't much time left to make any more preparations as school and I didn't break up until Thursday tea-time, 22 December. So instead of staying in bed later than usual on Sunday morning I had cooked breakfast by eight, then Elizabeth, Caroline and I took old baskets into the nearby woods. We wore scruffy old trousers, thick jumpers and wellingtons, with knitted caps to keep our ears warm. What heaven, plundering branches of deep red holly, gathering pine cones and fallen branches of trees for the fire!

Anticipation, and days outside, are almost more Christmasy than Christmas Day itself.

24

Christmas spirit

*A*lthough we all loved natural decorations in the home, Elizabeth was determined to be a bit more sophisticated with some of them. Armed with a bottle of silver glitter, bought from her spending money, she transformed some of the evergreens into a dazzling, shimmering gleam. Included in her scheme, if not by design, was the corner of Dad's best trousers and the tip of Prince's tail; when she swished the tail madly in the air it resembled a silver-topped walking-stick.

Maddening – on the last working Monday prior to Christmas we had unseasonably mild, rainy weather, and it was an exceptionally busy and hazardous morning on the crossing. There must have been a gas leak or something, as a great, gaping trench alongside my position on the shop side of the road, by the snicket, made it difficult to see oncoming traffic because of a huge lorry parked alongside. Men working on the trench, filling it in, meant that it was impossible for me to remain on the pavement, so I stayed in the centre, by the bollards, while buses, coal wagons, cars and vans swerved perilously close by me to avoid the trench operations. What a relief it wasn't foggy – I might have fallen into the trench and been buried alive!

The butcher's wife came staggering along to the bus stop carrying a whacking big case. 'I'm taking all me washing to t'launderette, getting the whole damned lot out of me way afore Christmas,' she explained after I'd enquired if she was leaving home.

'Isn't it very heavy?' I wanted to know, privately thinking what fools some are, risking heart attacks by hauling such weights when they probably had washing machines at home.

'Ah well,' she sniffed, with a queer logic of her own, 'it'll be lighter coming back.'

I think some go simply 'for a call', as Yorkshire folk describe sitting about swapping gossip. Watching the machines go round – how boring!

At half past nine on Thursday I caught the bus into town, not caring about being in my Lollipop uniform, as all the 'posh' types didn't turn out till much later on. It was lovely to be able to buy a few extra presents with my own money, including a packet of ten chocolate, silver-paper-covered Dutch boys and girls, at a shilling each, earmarked for the children's party I'd planned for Christmas Eve, a box of cheap crackers, a new diary for myself (7s 11d) and a few other odds and ends.

There was a parcel on the doorstep after the midday crossing. 'Do Not Open Till December 25th' was on the tag by the address. But who other than a saint could resist opening a parcel when in the house alone? And I prefer to look at gifts when no one else is watching my expressions. So I opened the expensive-looking bottle of perfume, from my brother Philip and his wife Audrey, for a pre-Christmas sniff. I then re-interred it beneath the wrappings and stuck the 'Do Not Open Till December 25th' tag down again. I was quite good at feigning surprise on birthdays and at Christmas.

Occasionally, when I was standing in the centre of the crossing, those waiting for me on the other side had to stare at me for what felt like an eternity, as if they were waiting for somebody or something to wind me up, like a clockwork toy. Sometimes there was no way at all of stopping the incessant flow of traffic, even when I put Lollipop on full view. When not one motorist, van or other vehicle was inclined to slow up, I was certainly not foolhardy enough to step out in front when they were in that defiant mood. A Lollipop pole was no match for tons of speeding machinery. Traffic was always worse, and most badly behaved, first thing in the morning and on the final crossing of the day.

Next Monday tea-time John the gardener was waiting at the other side, wanting to catch the four twenty bus into town. Although I kept making tentative moves to get off my 'island', it would have been suicide to try to. Even if the front vehicle stopped, the ones behind were belting down at such a pace I'd have been flattened like a pancake. Suddenly John lost all patience with the atrocious bad manners of the non-stop drivers.

'Hoi!' he yelled at the top of his voice, not caring who was listening, 'where the bloody hell are they all coming from?'

Next morning was most unlike what is expected of a December day – brilliant sunshine, warmth, blue skies. Who would want to swap my job on a day such as that? In between going down to the crossing I polished the furniture at home, sniffing the lavender aroma appreciatively. All the perfumes of Arabia couldn't have smelled better!

After 'garaging' Lollipop down the snicket at half past one, I walked on to the supermarket and had a chat with Tom, the other warden further down the road. He was nudging seventy, but as young-looking and active as a man twenty years younger. I told him so, which pleased him.

'I was in the Navy during the war, Hazel,' he explained. 'I couldn't stick an inside office job for love nor money. And I've never missed a day since starting on my crossing three years ago. It's all the ruddy central heating and preserved foods that ruins health. But they haven't sense to know it. They oughta get muffled up like thee and me, and face the elements. They'd feel a damned sight healthier if they did.'

We went on congratulating each other on our choice of work, then Tom asked, 'How are yer doing for Christmas presents on your patch?' He grinned broadly, his face still glowing with a healthy tan in darkest December. 'Vicar dropped me ten bob, I had another note from one o' t'school cleaners – ah started going down for me dinner yer know, after all. Saved a bit of money. A mother handed me a box of chocolates this morning, addressed to "Mr Warden". Best time o' t'year, this.'

Tom was obviously very 'chuffed' with all the attention.

'You'll have to bring some sort of waterproof collection box, with "Thank you" printed on it if it continues,' I said.

I was so pleased for him. He wasn't as lucky as me, living more or less on top of the job. Tom had a bus to get from home, but wouldn't accept a swap to a crossing nearer his home.

'I'm used to this one, I like it here. Know everybody. They know me. Coppers all know me, so do t'lorry and coal wagon drivers. Ah'm best where ah am. Besides,' he winked, 'if ah moved I'd miss all me Christmas presents, wouldn't I?'

Happiness, it seems, is fitting snugly into a niche – however ordinary – where you are appreciated and admired.

I woke later than usual on Wednesday. The morning was dark, so dark that our ears seemed deaf to the alarm clock. How I hated not having time to get a fire going for the children before having to race down to the crossing! Elizabeth had flown out without breakfast so as not to be late. So had Granville. Running down the lane, I asked passers-by, 'What time is it, please?' We needed a new clock – it kept going slow.

In a flurry of apprehension, I whizzed in front of traffic crossing the road to get Lollipop and get to the opposite side before children arrived. Fortunately, I wasn't late, but I might have been if I'd attended to the usual clearing out of the ashes from the grate and making a pot of tea. How awful it was shooting out with nothing to drink or eat first! A day begun in a hurry continues that way, with jobs crying out to be attended to from all angles.

It was party day for Caroline's class. We had less than half an hour at home, half past twelve till one, to grab a sandwich, yet she still preferred that to staying at school for dinner. But that day I'd had to go into town for shopping after the crossing duty ended at nine thirty. The fire still wouldn't light when I arrived home, so I rolled every bit of paper I could find into fire-lighters, wasted a whole box of matches, and chucked every bit of wood in sight on to the annoying black void. I trailed round the garden in search of firewood, but everything was wet through.

Caroline was cold, but I felt over-heated, having kept my coat on and dashing around. I wouldn't have bothered just for myself. Desperately I looked round the room for anything that might start a blaze in that grate. Becoming so frustrated and angry, I could have wrenched the table legs off and used those. Then a decision had to be made: continue ineffectually trying to make the fire light, or make something for Caroline to eat.

'Keep your coat on, Caroline,' I said. 'We'll have a glorious fire tonight. I'll buy a bundle of firewood at Nellie's.' Usually, gathering sticks ourselves, we had loads.

'Mummy, we have to take something to drink for the party, and label a spoon, saucer and plate with our names.'

'Oh, why didn't you say so last night?' Where was the cotton, and paper, to write 'Caroline Wheeler' on – and how to attach it to a plate? Saved – there was a small bottle of orange squash I'd bought for our children's party, but the top was so tight I knew Caroline could never unscrew it. Precious minutes ticked by towards one o'clock, and time for me to be at the crossing. Ah – the milkman clanked round to the back door. Agitated beyond all telling, I thrust the bottle at him.

'Richard, would you please mind undoing the top?' I'd run it under the hot water tap, but to no avail.

One calm, unhurried twist of the wrist, and hey presto – another problem solved. With trembling hands I poured the orange liquid into a Perspex tumbler and fastened the lid down firmly.

'You be writing your name on bits of paper while I try and fasten them on to the plates and spoon,' I called from the kitchen. Prince came rubbing round my legs, miaowing to be fed, nearly sending me headlong into the door. The cotton kept sliding off, and the more I hurried, the worse things were.

I didn't bother having anything to eat or drink myself, promising a leisurely snack after the crossing. Then I had to go.

'Try gluing the names on!' I shouted, slamming out of the front door at one minute to one. 'And even if you lose the flaming plates, I don't care.' Oh, for a flaming fire…

Situations like those made me almost hate being a Lollipop Lady, torn between having to leave Caroline and her unwillingness to stay for dinner as most others did. Yet how I wished there had been time for me to do things properly for her school party – a child is only a child for a very short time.

Yes. I made my mind up. Definitely. After such a morning. A tight pain caught my chest muscles as I raced to my post clutching the flipping pole.

I will give my notice in. Soon. There's nothing quite so exasperating as trying to do a number of jobs at once, within a limited time. Yes, I thought vehemently, as I stood like a robot with the damned crossing pole in my hand, 'Next year I'll make delicious, leisurely meals for Caroline and myself. It will be her last year at Junior school before she moves, hopefully, to the Girls Grammar School in town. Then she would *have* to stay. There wouldn't be time for her to come home. How strange if people could have read the thoughts racing through the mind of the Lollipop Lady on the crossing!

Besides, I wanted to help with her eleven-plus tests. I'd bought a couple of those intelligence test books, and I was dying to see if *I* was still capable of doing them, let alone Caroline!

Feeling in a more relaxed mood on the way home at half past one, I had a few words with Harry, gardener at the Old People's Home opposite our house.

'Hey, Hazel, come across when you've a minute. I'll show you through the old storage rooms in the cellars. And how to make real decorations from holly leaves and Irish yew!'

Harry made wreaths and garlands from the natural, abundant resources in the grounds, having acquired the art when learning gardening as a youth. He was known as 'a bit of a lad' with the local female population, so an encounter in the cellar could be interesting!

My good spirits were entirely back as I ate a cheese sandwich, liberally spread with chutney, and relaxed with lots of strong coffee. The fire was good-tempered at last, blazing cheerfully, making me wonder what it had all been about. Prince was fed and contented, and snoring in the armchair. Pulling on my wellingtons, I could have been a latter-day Lady Chatterley going to meet her lover!

'You've no need to go without fuel ever, Hazel,' Harry promised. 'There's enough logs here to make fires for many days to come. Glorious, old-fashioned, gorgeous-smelling log fires when the children come home from school. And Granville comes in from work.'

The Christmas Spirit was definitely around again. I hadn't noticed it before that harassing day. We'd be able to have real log fires over Christmas, and be the envy of all our centrally heated relatives and friends.

'Come and have a look through the cellars, all over a hundred years old. See, storage places for wines. Hooks on which pigs carcasses were hung in days when the Home was a private residence. That stone slab is where they were cut up.'

Jokingly, Harry grinned, 'Wonder how it would be on that!'

'Well, it's far too cold to bother finding out,' I laughed, moving towards the daylight and doorway. How interesting it all was. Sometimes things are of more interest nearer home than paying to trail all over.

As we walked back across the grounds, dozens of aged eyes stared at us from the windows of the Home. Next, Harry took me to view his wooden hut, where he fashioned the holly wreaths to decorate the Home. It was primitive on the outside, but bang up to date within, with photographs and magazine pictures of nude pin-ups all round the walls.

'How about one of you to join them?' he laughed

Letting that suggestion pass by, I watched him skilfully making part of a wreath before it was time for me to go home and get ready for being a Lollipop Lady again, not a potential nude pin-up.

Harry had told me to take my big shopping trolley across, and before going to the crossing I couldn't resist taking it to be filled with tulip bulbs, home-grown beetroot (far superior to that from a shop), Irish yew, branches, leaves and, for good measure, a pot of silver paint to decorate some of the leaves.

'I'll bring some logs across and leave them in your shed,' he promised. 'And when you've time, come over and I'll show you the main hall I decorated.'

When one recalls the workhouses of years ago, and the poor old people in them, living out their drab years and equally drab Christmas Days, that Home for the Aged, decked so beautifully for the festive season, was like a Fairy Palace in comparison.

25

End of term

I went across to see the Christmas decorations at the Home next day. Colourful paper trimmings festooned the high ceilings, and there were sprigs of mistletoe in abundance – pity there weren't the same amount of eligible suitors. But the more venturesome and romantically inclined old ladies might perhaps creep up on visiting vicars and doctors to recapture the thrill of a kiss beneath the mistletoe.

The pièce de résistance was Harry's creation of an outsize duck. It stood, head cocked inquisitively on one side, with a big golden 'egg' in front of it. The egg was a melon, painted gold by Harry in his hut. Then he had blown up a life-sized reindeer, made of balloons. An interestingly curved bough had been sprayed with silver and displayed in an earthenware container. The massive Christmas tree, decorated by Harry, would not have disgraced Buckingham Palace – what a tribute to his skill and devotion, giving so much time and happiness to those nearing the close of their lives. The tree dominated the place majestically, ablaze with glittering baubles and loops of tinsel. The whole effect was of an enchanted forest. With no disrespect to the ladies, they flitted to and fro like gnomes let loose in Fairyland, with Matron as Snow White among the dwarfs!

'He's a real grand 'un, our Harry,' enthused one resident. 'Marvellous!' chimed another, while one octogenarian danced ecstatically round Rudolph the Reindeer, clutching her handbag to her oversized chest and roaring with laughter, until Matron appeared and calmed her down.

Then it was time to go to the crossing, where old Mrs Jackson hobbled up to me, leaning heavily as usual on her walking-stick. I told her about the festive appearance of the Home, and how everyone seemed so happy there.

'Wouldn't you like to be there, with other people, instead of living along in the bungalow?' I asked her. 'We couldn't decorate our house in such a spectacular manner, and all that room, companionship – what do you think, Mrs Jackson?'

She sighed, unconvinced. 'Could you please telephone the coalman for me, Hazel, when you go back home? she pleaded wearily. 'I daren't leave the house to do any shopping in case he comes when I'm out.' She handed me a scrap of paper with the coalman's number.

'Are you *sure* you wouldn't prefer to live up there, opposite our house? No worries about heating, shopping for food in all kinds of weather – no garden to bother about, yet all those beautiful lawns and grounds to sit out in when it's summer?'

'Nay lass, ah'm too old to uproot mesen now,' and that was that.

Many independent souls still cling to the old, familiar way of life, harder though it is. I promised Mrs Jackson that I'd telephone the coalman as soon as I was home.

'Thanks love, I'm very grateful,' and the lonely figure moved slowly off back to her bungalow to wait for the coalman.

Then there was a lovely sight – seven lady horse-riders, erect in black coats and black riding hats, turned the corner of the lane on brown and grey horses. It was daydreaming time again! I imagined turning out like that at the crack of a bright dawn on Christmas or Boxing Day morning – though I'd be terrified if I actually had to attempt to get on to a horse! But to *look* like that! And after the hunt, galloping home for lunch, where a butler would serve me. Of course, I'd never want to hunt – and catch – a fox, or any other living creature. But what a picturesque sight a hunting scene makes, and how pleasant it was idly dreaming of what life *could* be like (and being paid for it) on the crossing in quiet moments.

Next morning, the last of the school year, was fine and sunny. I felt nostalgic and tearful, for almost three weeks the People on the Crossing would be going about their day-to-day business and I'd know nothing about it, unless I chanced to bump into them somewhere. Then again, next time I was there all the excitement of Christmas would be over. New Year, 1967, would have come and gone too, and by then I'd be so used to being an ordinary stay-at-home housewife that I may not want to take up the Lollipop pole of office again.

Yet there'd by pangs of regret at having no legitimate excuse for leaving indoor dust, and coming out into the sunshine as on that gloriously sunny day. As a Lollipop Lady I was a part of the mainstream of life, needed, of use. And even when standing doing nothing, simply enjoying the sunshine and blue skies – something I'd not make time for otherwise – I was getting paid for it. ('What is this life if, full of care, we have no time to stand and stare?')

Another aspect of not being able to get away from home was that there I was vulnerable when those horrible financiers came knocking at the door, demanding to see my husband. At least on the crossing I felt armed against their threats, and could forget them for a while. I was part of the teeming Cavalcade of Life – working and being paid, a contributory factor in getting the awful worry off our backs. At home there was more time to contemplate the terrible situation we were in. I managed to effectively push all that to the back of my mind when concentrating on traffic, and the difficulties experienced by others.

My thoughts were interrupted when a small boy thrust a paper bag, seasonable with Father Christmases, fir trees, snow and holly pictures, into my hand. He didn't say anything, just looked sheepish and shy.

'Oh!' I gasped, yanked out of my reverie. 'Oh, what is it? Thank you, thank you very much.' It was my very first Christmas present for being a Lollipop Lady, from one of my 'clients'. Tom wasn't the only one to be appreciated then!

My ego at that moment knew no bounds. I'd never thought anyone would actually buy *me* a Christmas present, apart from my family. I had time to open the bag before any other children appeared (patience not being one of my virtues). Inside I found one of those fancy lace-edged handkerchiefs in an ornate box, and a Christmas card on top. 'Just a small token in appreciation of your being so kind and helpful, whether the weather be fine, whether the weather be not. Have a Happy Christmas – and come back next year.'

I gulped. Me, who a moment ago had been plotting to escape from being a Lollipop Lady. And those bright tears, so close to the surface a few minutes ago, sprang quickly out and rolled slowly down my face.

Then another child handed me a lovely card, with a shy smile. The verse inside read: 'The bells chime out, To tell of Christmas, Their joyous note, Glad tidings bring. And may the echo of their gladness be in your heart, Till again they ring.' In someone's handwriting underneath: 'To the Lollipop lady. From Martin Strange (Mr). A small thank you.' The little boy was his son. It gave me a lovely warm glow to read those words. Then in a flash he came running back and pushed a packet into my hand. 'I forgot to give you this, as well. Dad said I mustn't forget.' Inside was half a pound of pork sausages. I was astounded – but delighted. They'd provide a tasty winter tea, with apple sauce and chips – big fat chips cooked in the chip pan. We could *all* share my present.

All the battering with the bad weather over the past weeks, all the soakings and frozen feet and fingers, all now seemed infinitely worthwhile. I felt a far greater happiness and satisfaction than in all the years I'd worked in offices in more 'status' jobs, though as a teenager I'd have hated telling boyfriends if I'd worked as a Lollipop Lady then! It was hardly the type of job to immediately impress people with. Yet after experiencing it, I realised what tenacity, intelligence, and, yes, even at times bravery was needed to be a successful one. I recalled one office where a couple of colleagues argued day in, day out, whether or not the windows should be open or shut. There on the crossing, there was no option. A school crossing warden had to accept what came, and could blame and argue with no one but the Almighty.

Young Howard skipped up to me. Handing me a box of chocolates he sang, 'Merry Christmas!' gleefully as I accepted the gift with many thanks. How trustworthy children can be – it would have been so easy for him to succumb to temptation and eat them himself!

I was beginning to feel like a Queen standing there accepting offerings of fealty from my subjects! Judith, almost seven, proudly handed me a folded white handkerchief in a brown paper sweet bag. Words tumbled over each other as she tried to remember all she had been instructed to say. 'My Mummy says thank you to the Lollipop Lady and hope you have a Happy Christmas.'

The rest of the day at the crossing was sprinkled with passers-by wishing me a Merry Christmas, over and over again. Yet no matter how many times those sentiments are echoed, they never lose their magic. Every time I heard them, something like a little sparkler shone inside me, like a beam of hope.

How I was enjoying myself! It was far better than being isolated at home with the cat, as in earlier years. Prince could only miaow 'Merry Christmas'.

Even normally miserable types had smiles twitching their lips that day, together with that indefinable light of Peace on Earth, Goodwill to all Men shining in their eyes. Surely one cannot deny that there is a different spirit abroad in the atmosphere at Christmas?

At half past one, after saying goodbye to Lollipop till three thirty, I set off jauntily to the supermarket, armed with two baskets that had waited by the wall until that duty ended. On the return journey my arms and shoulders ached, and I had to keep putting the heavy baskets down for a few minutes. It wasn't only the baskets – I also had two cardboard boxes fully wedged beneath my armpits. Oh to be one of those lucky shoppers with a car! I probably looked like what I felt, hopelessly deformed, exactly the opposite to the fairy on top of the Christmas tree.

Struggling up the lane, home in sight at last, I turned the key and sank into a chair with a glass of port from a bottle that Granville's firm had given him. Prince jumped on to my knee, and purred. She sensed there was something special in those baskets. Revived, there was the fun of gloating over boxes of crystallised ginger, Chinese figs, tins of plump Australian peaches and pears, tins of ham and pork, and the pleasure of arranging them invitingly in the kitchen cabinet, like a squirrel hoarding nuts for winter.

In no time at all the clock was pointing to three twenty, and I set off for the very last crossing duty of the year. I hadn't been there a couple of minutes before dear old Mrs Jackson appeared, clutching a white paper bag in her brown-gloved hand.

'See luv, give these to Elizabeth and Caroline from me. For Christmas.' How touched I was at the old lady's thoughtfulness, and thanked her very much indeed.

'Are you fixed up for Christmas yet?' I asked anxiously.

'Yes thank you, I am. They wrote – eventually,' she smiled bleakly.

'Well then, you must come up one day and have tea with us before school begins again – don't forget.' I didn't hold out any hopes that she would. 'There'll be nothing to worry about. Granville will come down for you and see you safely home again in the evening,' I promised. How I wanted *her* to feel wanted again…

'We'll see. I'll look forward to that. Anyhow, a Merry Christmas to you all – ay, I do wish my Luther was here, that I do.'

'I'm sure he'll be with you – in spirit – dear Mrs Jackson, and I do hope you have as good a Christmas as possible. Under the circumstances. Thank you for the chocolates,' I called after her. Inquisitive as usual I peeped into the bag – Maltesers. I popped them into my shopping bag and zipped it up. How time flew – soon it would be half past four, and time to put Lollipop down the snicket. Sentimentally I held her a few inches from me, and gazed at her. I wished somehow I could give *her* a present. How mean for all the gifts to be mine, yet Lollipop was the other half of the crossing duo. She had only had her face washed once in all those months since we had been partners on the crossing; when the crossing cleaner man had stretched over from his ladder dealing with the bollards in the middle of the road, he had given Lollipop a brief wipe over, each side. Poor, hardworking pole…

'A Merry Christmas to you, Lollipop,' I whispered, holding her against my coat. 'I'll miss you.'

Standing as it did, about the same height as myself, I'd come to think of the pole as my Colleague of the Crossing, like another person, there to listen to and absorb all my comments when nobody else was about.

The run-up to Christmas was accelerating. Lorry drivers honked their horns, poking their heads out of cabs and yelling 'Merry Christmas, Lollipop – got any mistletoe?' I blew kisses to them as they passed by. What fun it was, flirting again, especially as I was in no danger of the flirting escalating to anything else!

The Infant School children's happiness and excitement was translucent as they jostled to be first out of the snicket. Pump bags swung merrily, tiny pointed paper party hats sat drunkenly on small heads. The boys didn't know what to do or say next to see who could be silliest and cause most laughs.

'Merry Christmas, Mr Lamp Post!' roared one, giving it a playful kick.

'Merry Christmas, silly old school!' shouted another, turning to look down the snicket and waving.

'Merry Christmas, Mr Snowflake!' yelled another.

Their exhilaration was infectious, releasing the 'child' I once was. I began thinking up equally ridiculous things to offer Season's Greetings to.

'Merry Christmas, crossing! Merry Christmas, world!'

With the children I joined hands and danced on the pavement, snowflakes brushing our faces. It was *real* fun – better than a tipsy office party, where some needed drinks before they could let go of their usual staid workaday self. The children and I had captured the Spirit of Christmas, right there on the cold whitening pavement. It would be with us until we met again in the New Year.

It was with mixed feelings – elation and despondency alternating – that I saw the last child disappearing from view. Tomorrow I would be able to really get down to the housework and preparations for our Christmas without constant interruptions throughout the day. Lollipop and I crossed to the snicket, empty now. Looking round so that nobody would see me, I drew the pole towards me, and kissed her 'au revoir'. With tears rolling down my cheeks I left her there, snow already lightly covering her face.

26

'Twas the night before Christmas...'

Next morning I was an eager beaver in old trews, jumper and flatties. With carols on the radio as I worked, I washed the woodwork in the front room ('lounge' sounds so pretentious, I think), catching the odd spider that ventured out from the fireplace, and polished the furniture for the last time before Christmas. Elizabeth and Caroline helped, in fits and starts, but more often than not played games or with Prince. Sometimes they made presents out of odds and ends to eke out having something for everyone – maybe a plant pot stand made with old bits of wool, using a French knitting set.

We went across into the wood for a fresh supply of scarlet holly berries to add the finishing festive touch. Then the room was ready at last for the following day, Christmas Eve. We'd invited some of the children I'd become friends with on the crossing, the poorer ones, and Grandma and Grandad had been roped in to help. Six o'clock was the time for the party to commence, and the Hungarian lady, Anna, was thrilled that her little daughters Diane and Elizabeth had been invited.

'My husband and I will be able to go to the pub now, and I promise they won't turn up without shoes!' she laughed.

Two of the little girls who lived on the main road, and whose parents had a large family but a small income, were also delighted to have been asked, the older children thinking themselves too old for a children's party, being teenagers. So it wouldn't be all girls, I'd asked one boy, who said yes, if his pal could come too. So that was all right.

The first guests timidly knocking at the front door were Mary and Barbara, who lived in one of the old terrace houses on the main road. Mary's coat was too small, and some four or five inches of thin summery dress showed bedraggled beneath it. Buttons didn't meet across the little flat chest, yet it was a bitterly cold night, crisp with frost. Mary's nose end was redder than the holly berries on the hall stand, and on her feet were open sandals.

'Come in, pets, get to the fire,' I urged, putting my arms round them and ushering them into the glowing welcome of the front room. Chestnuts were arrayed in front of the blazing log fire, and fairy lights twinkled instead of the ordinary lights. It isn't money that makes a wonderful party, but including those who otherwise would not go anywhere, and making them all feel that they are the most important people, the most wanted, in the world.

There were two pouffes either side of the fire. 'Sit on those, help yourselves to nuts – and Elizabeth and Caroline will see to your drinks.'

Mother, our pianist, made a fuss of one and all in between playing requests for favourite carols. The children adored the home-made ginger beer, never having had any before. There were sandwiches, a whopping trifle, Christmas cake and cheese. Prince, full length on the rug, jumped every time a chestnut exploded, and hissed back at them.

I loved knitting on winter nights, and had made lots of easy wool caps from double-knitting left over from jumpers I'd made, one for every child, wrapped in festive paper and in a sack with other labelled odds and ends. Grandad dressed as Santa Claus, and was there to hand out prizes for quiz winners and the child having the most interesting story to tell about other Christmases, the one who knew who the Prime Minister was, the child who won by singing a carol – everyone was a winner, I made sure of that.

'We've never been to a proper party like this before, wiv candles,' breathed Mary in her shabby summer dress. 'It's luvly, isn't it?'

Pass the Parcel is always a winner, especially with a Grandma playing the piano and stopping at the exact moment to give all an equal chance.

Then everybody stood round the piano for community carol singing, and balloons were batted to and fro, the fireguard keeping them away from the crackling bright fire. 'Good King Wenceslas' was played with Granville as the king, the little boys his pages, and plenty of winter fuel in the open wicker basket full to the brim with logs courtesy of Harry, the gardener from the Home opposite.

While everybody was enjoying themselves I sneaked upstairs to look through the wardrobes in the children's bedroom. Good, there was a warm coat of Caroline's, too small for her now, as well as a number of dresses, skirts and jumpers that I'd been thinking of giving away.

I pushed them all into a bolster case and took them downstairs, placing it behind the front door. Grandma was in her element performing her party piece, 'Burlington Bertie' ('from Bow, ho-ho') to screams of laughter and delight from the children. Crackers were pulled, we played Consequences and Truth or Dare, and nobody missed the television at all.

And none of us wanted the night to end. We listened to The Worst Christmas and The Best Christmas as we sat in a circle in the firelight, and there were small prizes for the ones voted best.

Grandma playing 'Silent night', 'The First Nowell', and all the other beloved carols as the children munched and thought up stories, then brains worked overtime for the game 'Town, Country, County, River, Tree, Animal, Bird, Girl's name, Boy's name', which all had to begin with the same letter. There were ten points for each right answer, divided if more than one child had the same one.

While they were thinking, a little frown came over Mary's face.

'Me Dad smokes like a chimney, Mrs Wheeler. Barbara and me wanted to buy him some cigarettes for his Christmas present. But we hadn't enough after buying our Mam a box of Turkish Delight.' She looked at the chestnuts. 'Do you think – if there are any over, do you think we could take a few for Dad? Please?' I'll never forget the pathetic look on her little face. If I'd had a thousand pounds to give, how wonderful it would have been to give it to her!

'Well, I'm glad you've reminded me, Mary,' Granville smiled at the little girl. 'I've had so many cigarettes given from work, even a few cigars. I can easily spare some for your Dad.'

Oh, what a transformation – joy unbounded shone in Mary's eyes. 'Oh thank you, thank you, Mr Wheeler – I can't wait to see Dad's face on Christmas morning. Thank you!' echoed by her sister Barbara. How very true, that giving *is* better than receiving!

How glad I was that circumstances had led me to work as a Lollipop Lady, if only to give a bit of pleasure to children such as Mary and Barbara.

The boys' parents arrived about eleven to take them home. They had had a super evening, and thanked us so much for looking after them.

But nobody turned up for Mary and Barbara. 'Mam will be looking after the baby,' explained Barbara. 'We'll be all right walking down the lane by ourselves. I'm used to looking after our Mary.'

'Oh no you won't – Elizabeth and Caroline's Daddy will take you. There might be a lot of drunks about,' I said. 'Besides, I've something else for you, and it's too heavy for you to carry yourselves.' I brought the bolster into the room. 'Anything in there to fit you?'

Happiness! Mary brought out the winter red coat, which buttoned right up to the neck, two knitted jumpers, one in bright blue, the other scarlet, two pairs of mittens, tartan skirts, ribbed tights, slippers.

'Try them on – let's have a fashion parade,' I suggested. The clothes fitted perfectly.

'Can I walk down the road in the coat please?' Mary asked.

''Course you can, and we'll put the other in the sack,' I said. Elizabeth, conscious that the older girl, Barbara, hadn't a 'new' coat, shyly said, 'Mummy – that duffle coat of mine, it's getting a bit tight…'

Well, the sales would be starting on Boxing Day, and there might be enough to get a new one for Elizabeth. 'Oh yes, I'd forgotten. Bring it down, see if it fits Barbara.' It did. What a wonderful Christmas Eve we had!

Granville added the cigarettes and a couple of cigars to the bolster case, and finally, in a euphoria of Christmas giving, I cut a whopping hunk of Christmas cake for the two little girls to take home with them, including the tiny brown, red-breasted toy robin from the icing.

With wisps of jet black hair curling on to the red coat and a red knitted cap pulled well down over her ears, Mary looked the epitome of Christmas, with the decorated tree behind her. Barbara was at a loss for words, in her 'new' warm navy duffle coat, but her expression said it all.

'And *we* can't thank you all enough. We have loved having all of you here, and want you to come again some time.'

They had contributed so much to the success of the party, with quaint little stories about their family, and the funny little songs they had sung – above all, the obvious enjoyment.

I knew that all the work I'd put into making the party being a success, all the extra shopping, planning of games, wrapping the huge Pass the Parcel, wrapping small prizes, had been so worthwhile. Indeed, it had been our best Christmas Eve for years.

As Granville summed it up after taking Mary and Barbara safely home, 'We haven't much money, but we do have fun,' as we kissed beneath the mistletoe in the hallway. Yes, we still loved each other, despite all the worries and insults occasionally hurled.

The other children had thoroughly enjoyed themselves as well. But with Mary and Barbara, I felt as though I had taken their small grubby hands in mine, and led them straight into Fairyland, or as near to Fairyland as I could manage. I remembered again how stars seemed reflected in their eyes as I lifted the star-spangled fairy from the top of the Christmas tree before they left.

'Will you give this to your baby sister?' I asked, adding it to the things in the bolster case. I wanted to go on giving to those two poor little waifs for ever.

And to Granville too. How dependable, how good he was, as he had taken their hands and led them, slipping and slithering down the icy garden path, the bolster tied round his neck with string so he could keep tightly hold of the children's hands. Voices rang out on the Christmas air, 'Thank you, thank you, we've had a lovely party.'

Grandma and Grandad had gone home in a taxi, shouting 'See you tomorrow, Happy Christmas!' as it sped away into the night. Diane and

Elizabeth, the Hungarian girls, were still there, laughing and talking with our Elizabeth, and Caroline.

'Can we stay a bit longer, please?' they asked. 'Mummy and Daddy went out with their friends, and said we'd to wait till they came for us.'

I'd given an evening, rather than an afternoon, children's party on purpose, so that those parents who never could go out together on an evening, having nobody to look after the children, would be able to.

'Stay as long as you like,' Granville and I said. 'We don't want to go to bed leaving a big fire like this – it needs to die down a bit first.'

On the stroke of midnight we heard excited voices at the front door and banging, then a tipsy kind of singing: 'We wish you a Merry Christmas, We wish you a Merry Christmas and a Happy New Year'. We opened the door and Anna and her big, broad husband almost fell into the hallway, giggling foolishly.

'I think you need to go straight home to bed,' he laughed, steadying Anna. 'Mixed too many drinks,' he explained.

'You mean she put lemonade in her Coke?' asked Diane.

'Yes, something like that,' agreed their Dad, winking.

It was the early hours of Christmas morning before I pulled the blankets round and switched out the light, and was hardly in dreamland when I was roused by the local church choir carolling 'Christians, Awake' in the lane below. I could hear snowflakes softly failing against the window panes. I snuggled deeper down into the blankets, curling, spoonlike, behind Granville, who was snoring, oblivious to those urging him to awake.

There were, as always, many sad people that Christmas – but I was happy in the knowledge that at least two small girls, Mary and Barbara, would have gone to bed happy. Then into my mind came a vision of poor Lollipop. All alone down that snicket – was she missing me, I wondered?

I didn't seem to have been asleep two minutes before Elizabeth and Caroline, tousle-headed and clutching bulging long black stockings, burst into our bedroom, clambering into bed and shaking the blankets to rouse us from sleep. 'He's been – he's been!' they shouted, knowing full well that 'he', translated, was us, but keeping up the beloved old tradition to please me.

After the dark clouds of night had rolled away we had a late breakfast and exchanged presents. When I drew the curtains there was a small pool of water on the inside windowsills, and a thin covering of snow outside.

'One day, when I'm rich, we'll have double glazing and put an end to all this dreariness, mopping up with towels every flipping window,' I sighed.

By midday there was brilliant sunshine and blue sky, with the tag end of snow, the merest suspicion of it, still on the ground. Weatherwise it was a perfect Christmas Day, that year of 1966 in Yorkshire. Not having a car, and Mother's home being two bus rides away, we had to have a taxi. Grandad, my stepfather, had the new card table out ready to take on the children at a few games.

Boxing Day was spent with the other grandparents, Granville's Mother and Dad. We were invited to a friend's for tea on the following day. What a treat for me not having to worry about how to afford a turkey that year, and knowing that we wouldn't be feeding turkey to Prince for the next goodness knows how long.

On New Year's Eve we had a party at our house for the grown-ups: Grandmas and Grandads, and friends from the Authors' Circle in Huddersfield, all boosting each other's confidence that maybe next year one of us may have 'made the grade' and had a book published. Last, but not least, of our guests was Elizabeth's piano teacher. An adroit move that, providing a pianist on the spot!

I had asked everyone to bring a true story about their happiest Christmas, to be read as we basked in the firelight and the lights from the Christmas tree, and lit candles, my favourite form of lighting. I gave a prize for the one voted the most entertaining.

When the church bells pealed out, ringing in the New Year, 1967, we switched on the television. A choir was singing 'Time like an ever-rolling stone bears all her sons away'. What happens to daughters, I wanted to know.

27

Ring in the new

New Year's Day, 1967, dawned bright with a blue sky, and was warm enough to work upstairs. I had to wait for a reasonably mild day to bear working upstairs, not having central heating, though I wasn't really sorry about the latter – I think it makes people soft!

Mother arrived in the afternoon for tea and a closer examination of the new Christmas games and toys. We had a pleasant relaxing day sitting round the fire, the children sewing dresses for the dolls while I knitted some of a new pullover for Granville. Grandad came for Grandma in the evening and played Monopoly with Elizabeth and Caroline for what seemed like hours. They were all too involved in speculating, buying and selling to worry about supper.

On Thursday morning we went into town to collect my holiday pay of £1 10s, then to Bradford shopping for a change. Granville had been given a £5 voucher from a firm he deals with, to spend at a certain Bradford store, while the money Elizabeth and Caroline had been given from relations was almost leaping from their purses. Caroline spent all hers on a toy sewing machine, adequate to make dolls' clothes with. But Elizabeth, after great deliberation, came home with all her money still intact.

'I'm going to wait till the sales start, then I'll get more for my money,' she diplomatically declared.

We carried the bulb bowls up from the cellar one morning. 'Wonder which will flower first, daffodils or hyacinths,' I said, placing the bowls in different rooms.

Elizabeth had been given a sculpture set for one of her presents. One rainy afternoon she had a go at modelling the ballerina, scooping wet plaster into the rubber mould.

'I can't get it out again, it's stuck,' she agonised long after it should have been set. She got a lump of plaster in her eye, then eventually only the lower bit of the ballerina emerged from the cast. Hoping for some miracle, she left the other half in the mould for a few days before it was thrown into the dustbin.

'I'd hoped you would start modelling small ornaments that Nellie might sell in her shop, and in no time at all pay off all our debts.' Another idea bit the dust! Still, it was the hope of one day hitting on a great idea that could deliver us from those moneylenders that kept us going.

At least we had a different-coloured carpet, now white speckled. Perhaps our fortune would change as the New Year of 1967 got under way. It looked as though working on the crossing wasn't ending just yet. Meanwhile, Roddy, the tomcat from the bungalow opposite, loved me being at home all day, frequently appearing on the back windowsill after a heroic leap up. Then I opened the window for him to share the warmth of the fire and a sleep in the doll's pram, which I daren't do when I was working, unless he was already asleep in it before I left the house.

On 9 January it was easy to tell that school was about to begin next day by all the wailing and weeping – a change in routine is a good thing in one respect, but it takes some getting used to having a timetable to adhere to afterwards.

Elizabeth couldn't sleep. 'I haven't done my homework – not even begun it,' she moaned. It was past midnight, a bit late to say that. I didn't have much patience – there had been plenty of opportunity. Then Caroline had a pain, she didn't know where – and felt vaguely sick. After listening to her heartbroken sobbing for ages I went into her bedroom.

'Shall I ring for a doctor?' I wanted to know.

'He can't do anything,' Caroline replied. ''Cos the door is stiff sometimes in a morning after you've gone to the crossing and I'm worried in case I can't open it and come to school. Especially when there's an exam.'

Oh dear, poor Caroline! She had never mentioned it before, but it was true. Sometimes it took all my ingenuity to open the damned door, no matter how much oil was put on it. It was worse in bad weather, but old and decrepit at the best of times.

'Is *any* job worth having a child upset for?' I asked Granville as I snuggled back into bed.

It would have been foolish to leave the door unlocked after I went out. Early January mornings are still dark, and anyone could sneak into the house. Then I started to cry at the thought of having to return to being a Lollipop lady, with Caroline upset at home – how I wished we had enough money not to have to make such decisions!

I'd seriously doubted my ability to get out of the warm bed that morning when the alarm clock shrilled at seven, after the leisurely pace of life during the holidays. Before leaving to take up my duties on the crossing for the Spring Term, I kept opening, shutting, and opening again the front door to show Caroline that it was all right that day. Passers by must have thought I couldn't make up my mind whether to go out or stay in.

The road was icy and slippery as I hurried down the lane wearing my uniform again. I hoped I wouldn't fall full length in front of a vehicle as I crossed backwards and forwards with groups of children. How ridiculous, calling this the Spring Term, with such conditions underfoot! It was like trying to walk upright on a sheet of glass. But like magazines, schools seem to prefer keeping ahead.

Brown Grandad and Beverley held on to Lollipop as we teetered across. 'Gad, never thought I'd have to be an ice-skater at my damned age!' he muttered, while Beverley kept up a regular shriek of 'Oh … oh…'

'I think it's time I packed this ice-skating lark in,' I replied, skidding over the crossing for the umpteenth time until everything warmed up slightly before nine.

In those darkest mornings of January it was so much harder to drag myself out of bed – better leave the job now before that happened. I'd be for ever condemned if through my negligence, not being there, a child was injured… Many mornings I had to hang about doing nothing until about a quarter to nine, with no children appearing until then. But I knew if I just happened to be late once, then something would occur to blight my record of reliability. Parents, teachers, police, education authorities, everyone would then pour scorn on me. There would be headlines in the local paper: 'Staying in bed more important than looking after children', 'Lollipop Lady causes child to lose its life'. Oh God, I daren't go on!

Mrs Morrison turned up.

'I wonder what other job I could get to bring in a regular bit of money without such a big responsibility?' I worried.

'They were advertising for a part-time bingo attendant at the Palace,' she laughed, knowing that wasn't my scene at all. Then Irish Mrs Murphy came up and joined in the conversation.

'Ee, the other night I was there and an old feller won the jackpot – went as white as a sheet. Trembling so much he could neither stand up or write his name. We thought he was going to die of a heart attack before he had any benefit from it.'

'What's the pay?' I asked, not wanting to appear snooty.

'Three shillings and sixpence an hour,' Mrs Murphy said proudly.

I could never understand people who, willy-nilly, spent money on bingo night after night, then, if they won a few pounds occasionally, thought it was wonderful. The game itself held no interest for me either. I preferred games that weren't just founded on luck, but by using one's brains. So, not even for the magnificent sum of three and six an hour was I ever going to swap being a Lollipop Lady. On the crossing, at least there was always a variety of people to talk to, and nobody puffing cigarette smoke in a garishly furnished bingo hall.

Stephen, a sixth-former, walked up to me with a large hold-all crammed with text books.

'You look as though you've had a busy time, Stephen,' I observed. He grinned wryly.

'Haven't opened one all holiday – but I do think they look impressive, don't you?'

I enjoyed many stimulating conversations with Stephen and others like him when they were waiting for a bus!

At midday I noticed some workmen felling trees across in the grounds of the Home. They downed tools and leaned on the tree stumps to gaze at me in curiosity as I came out of the front door, wearing my heavy navy trousers, wellingtons, the navy beret and heavy white warden coat over a long woollen cardigan for extra warmth. Their prolonged stares made me feel like a circus exhibit and I felt myself beginning to blush. I wished I dare call out, 'Stare, stare, you big fat bear, stare till your mother comes home from t'fair!'

They then strolled slowly up to me, wide grins creasing their weather-beaten faces.

'Hey, Lollipop, give us a kiss!' One attempted to put his arm round my waist. 'Those old women in there are making us feel sex-starved.' His pal jerked nearer, hands moving in corduroy pockets. 'How about holding *my* lollipop, eh?'

I swerved to avoid them and ran as fast as I could to the bottom of the lane. Manual workers take a delight in accosting females – one is bad enough, but when in a gang it's most embarrassing. I dreaded the idea of being the object of sexual suggestions on my way home again. I enjoy fun, but not coarseness. It wasn't as though I liked the look of any of them, either. Some seem to think because they are outdoor workers, and not in the more prosaic suit, collar and tie, lewd remarks are more or less expected of them.

Mrs Costa pottered up. 'Ah'll just have a word with you, Hazel, while you've nothing on,' was her opening gambit, meaning that she had nothing to attend to that would prevent her gossiping for a while. Some have strange ways of speech...

It was about quarter past one. She folded her arms defiantly. 'That blessed coalman of ours has let us down again,' she exploded. 'He's a right so and so.'

I took my opportunity. 'Why don't you walk back up the lane with me and gather some logs for the fire until he turns up? They're felling trees opposite our house.'

'Oh, what a good idea!' she glowed. 'Hold on a bit while I nip back home and find a couple of old sacks.'

When two of us appeared, not just me, the workmen refrained from cat-calls. Being an 'older women' like Mrs Costa had its compensations, not the least being that they seem to be exempt from those ear-piercing wolf whistles, grotesque hand signs and other suggestive stuff that is the stock in trade of a lot of outdoor workers. Their attitude was different altogether. We were treated as normal people, not sex objects. They couldn't have been more helpful.

'Open t'bag, luv, we'll soon have it filled,' one offered, chucking in sticks, logs and other kindling for Mrs Costa, smiling amiably.

I filled the other sack, thoroughly enjoying helping and loving being in the fresh air. Our taking some of the debris of cut-down branches helped them too, as they had more room to move around. Mrs Costa made two or three trips home, coming back gleefully for refills. She giggled happily.

'Bugger the coalman now,' she chortled. 'Ee, ah'm fair glad ah went across to have a word with our Lollipop!'

As often happens, all's well that ends well!

'Have you had a good Christmas?' I asked Brown Grandad as he trotted towards me, holding Beverley firmly by the hand. It was the last crossing of the day already.

'Aye, but she hasn't.' He indicated the rather wan-faced Beverley. 'Poor little devil's had a carbuncle and spent most of Christmas sitting on a potty over boiling water.'

At my look of astonishment, Brown Grandad explained. 'It was in an awkward spot you see. Poor kid couldn't sit down.'

'I think I remember Beverley having an abscess not long ago,' I recalled.

Brown Grandad nodded his head. 'Aye, she did. Trouble nowadays, they don't get to t'root of the trouble at first. Just pump drugs into 'em to camouflage the immediate problem. But that's no good. Simply drugging badness from the surface, and pushing it back into the body. Badness will find its way out somehow. Ay dear, it was a bit of a queer spot to choose, wasn't it, chick?' He grinned down fondly at his granddaughter, who nudged him to shut up. No girl likes her personal anatomy being discussed on the Public Highway.

Brown Grandad switched the subject to himself as there was time to spare. 'We've had one or two near do's this Christmas ourselves, t'wife and me. Some of those blasted bus drivers simply refuse to stop when they see anybody coming. We were coming back from t'supermarket, and t'bags being extra heavy we decided to hop on a bus. Wife got on, having her hands free, 'cos she'd handed her basket over to me. Then I made a grab for t'bus pole – and missed the ruddy thing. He'd rung off as well. There were t'wife, crying and gesticulating on t'side seat. Ee, we were in a mess! Me flat on me belly an all.'

I sympathised, but he still hadn't finished the tale. He chuckled, wiping tears of laughter from his eyes with the back of his hand.

'There's allus a funny side to it. Usually is. T'wife wasn't going to be whirled away on her own, leaving me flat on me belly on t'ground, wi' tins o' peaches and teacakes and God knows what spread all round me. Oh no, whether t'bus was in motion or not, she wasn't staying on it by herself. When I looked up from t'grit, there was me missus lying flat on her belly at t'side o' me, hat all cocked to one side and two great bust knees bleeding out of her torn stockings.'

'What on earth did you do?' I wanted to know.

'Got up, of course. Nay lass, ah said to me wife, nay lass, tha shouldn't a bothered.'

I laughed with Brown Grandad.

'True love proves itself more in sickness than in health,' I told him.

Beverley tugged the edge of her hero's coat. 'Come on, Grandad, the bell will be going.'

'So long then, Lollipop – Happy New Year!' called Brown Grandad as they stumbled off down the snicket. His shoulders were still heaving with merriment as he turned to wave, tripping over a stone slightly as he and Beverley disappeared from view.

In another quiet period between taking anyone over to the other side of the crossing I ruminated about time. How quickly it flies, and children grow up. It had seemed no time at all since Beverley had been a chubby one-year-old in her pram. I remembered having seen Brown Grandad – as I thought of him since seeing them on the crossing – pushing the baby in it. And I didn't know them then. In a few more years Beverley might be dating one of the little boys now wearing short pants, who pulled her curly hair. She wouldn't thank her Grandad then for recalling that Christmas carbuncle!

Yes, time does indeed fly. Elizabeth was telling us about her school friend Susan. Twelve years old, Susan had already had a proposal of marriage from one of the boys in her class.

'Have you ever been asked?' I queried our elder daughter.

'Oh yes,' she replied nonchalantly.

'Who by?' my interest quickening. (If she married a millionaire, we might, conceivably, have paid off the moneylenders if he helped us out, in a few years' time...)

'The same boy,' was the nonplussing reply.

The weather continued mild for January. It often fools us. If we enjoy a mild first month of the year, it often has to be paid for later on, as I remembered from the previous February, when I first started working on the crossing. Even so, early mornings, though mild later, were pretty treacherous. The Matron of the Old People's Home passed me, her arm in a sling.

'Broke it coming down the lane a few days ago,' she explained. 'Easy as that. One minute right as rain, next incapacitated for weeks.' I wondered if the accident had been made more likely because of children making sledge runs down the pavements, creating worse conditions for walking. Sometimes there wasn't an inch of pavement free from sledge marks, making the whole surface worse than a skating rink. I'm not a killjoy, but do believe that fields and hills are the places for sledging, not public pathways.

All the glitter and magic of Christmas had disappeared from Nellie's and the other small shops across the road. Instead of tiny fir trees, dolls and fairy lights in Nellie's front window, there were signs of spring cleaning: brushes, dishcloths, tins of Mansion polish and detergents, lavatory cleaners. Everything, including life, had taken on a beige, neutral appearance. The fascination had gone.

The Christmas Spirit of Goodwill had disappeared from some of the youngsters too. It was back to fighting and bullying among the boys. A couple of lads tumbled out of the snicket, fists clenched, shirts torn, pummelling each other like professional boxers, and taking no notice when adults attempted to part them. They were like mad dogs. It was the last crossing of the day, and I was on the side of the snicket. I pushed Lollipop between them. They ignored it. Then Mike's watch, a Christmas present from his Dad, fell to the ground, his opponent's boots smashing it to pieces. The shock of that ended the fight. It was hopeless trying to piece together the fragments of glass. The loss of his treasured watch hurt the boy more than any physical torment he'd suffered at the fists of the other. It was a crestfallen couple of small boys that dragged their feet in the direction of their homes.

Little Sheila tugged my sleeve. 'Miss – do you know the story of Fatty and Thinny?'

'Go on, say it,' giggled her duffle-coated friend.

Sheila took a deep breath. What obscenity was I to hear...? The girls nudged each other.

'Fatty and Thinny were in bed,
Fatty rolled over and Thinny were dead.'

Greatly excited at their daring, the two children clutched hands and shrieked with delight, as I laughed with them. Then, with Lollipop, I stepped out into the road to stop the oncoming traffic; a number 73 bus rolling over them – or me – would be far worse than the fate of Thinny.

They were silly stories, yet I knew that when I finally packed the job in, those were some of the aspects of being a Lollipop Lady I'd miss: being a part of the innocence of childhood, putting aside the grown-up world for a brief space every day.

A few days later I made up my mind finally, and gave my notice in at the Education Office. They begged me to reconsider my decision.

'We simply can't get wardens, Mrs Wheeler – do stay. Only pensioners seem to want to bother with the job.'

If I'd have hesitated for even one moment I may have wavered. I hate disappointing anyone.

'I'm sorry, but I do want to write – and there's so little time. When I'm watching the clock all day I can't concentrate. One day I hope to write a book about being a Lollipop Lady and then lots will want to do the job,' I promised.

28

The cavalcade is over

I knew that if I stayed any longer I'd be too emotionally attached to the people I'd come to know, and I'd never leave. Now I wanted the challenge of writing. Would I be able to earn as much writing as I earned as a school crossing warden, small as that amount was? But I believe we should follow our secret star, our innermost ambitions. Otherwise the world will be filled with millions of dissatisfied grumblers along Life's Way. Many have no option but to keep on the same old route. That must be terrible.

Caroline had a guilty look on my last but one morning. 'I hope nobody is in the house when you get back,' she greeted me at the crossing. 'The front latch wouldn't open again, so I'd to come out of the back, and leave the door unlocked. I couldn't find the big key anywhere.'

It was another eleven-plus examination morning. Now the die was cast, and I'd given in my notice, how glad I was that particular difficulty could never arise again. At half past nine I dashed up home quicker than ever, and looked under all the beds. No intruder – nothing there except fluff, so I was safe. Looking out of the bedroom window I saw that the workmen across the road had something more to occupy them than shouting after the opposite sex. To my dismay, they were hacking down the ancient chestnut tree – I used to adore gazing out of the window at it and its beautifully coloured leaves. Another sad goodbye.

But the old chestnut tree had great tenacity. Its roots went deep. The service of a crane had to be enlisted to force the remaining trunk of the tree from the ground, but all to no avail. The ground sank, but the roots stayed. Finally both crane and man left, completely defeated by nature. I gave a silent cheer!

On the crossing I was a listening ear to what parents thought about the education system. One of the Infant children's mothers was most dissatisfied about the way in which children starting school were being taught.

'It's all play and no work nowadays,' she told me. 'They don't teach them to read now,' she grumbled. 'I'd almost prefer an illegitimate child to an illiterate one,' she stormed.

How relieved I was that our two daughters had learned to read before the new methods were adopted. That irate mother had every reason to be annoyed. There's plenty of time for play at home. Mothers were feeling frustrated recalling what *they* could do, academically, at the same age.

Approaching four o'clock the mild weather suddenly changed, and a cold wind blew up. I turned up my collar against the blasts sweeping round the corner.

'Atta sweating mate?' a raucous voice shouted above the wind. A coalman, grinning from ear to ear, leaned over from his position on top of a wagon full of coal. How I enjoyed that easy camaraderie, the friendly familiarity on 'my' crossing. It was strange to realise that next week, if he came across me in 'normal' clothes, not the navy beret, white plastic mac and wellington boots, not forgetting my pole of office, dear old Lollipop, he probably wouldn't recognise me and certainly wouldn't address me as 'mate'! I'd been 'mate' to more men since becoming a Lollipop Lady than ever I'd considered possible. Neither would I be addressed as 'Mrs Warden' any more, as the brash Secondary Modern schoolboy addressed me a little while later.

'Can you tell us reet time, Mrs Warden?' he drawled, rubbing against me, encircling my waist with his arm.

Oh gosh, what had I done? Next week I'd have lost my identity on the crossing, and be back to an ordinary housewife again. Had I made a mistake?

My last day as a Lollipop Lady dawned. Putting on my uniform for the final time, I felt down in the dumps. A chapter in my life – one I could never have envisaged happening – was about to close.

However, as the day wore on, little incidents cropped up that lifted my depression and made me begin to look forward to becoming a free agent once again. Not least, there was another dicey encounter with the huge Alsatian that had tried to cannibalise my nose a few weeks before. The lady who owned it was quite unperturbed.

'Oh, don't back away from him, Mrs Wheeler. He's a lot better now. Much more confidence in himself.'

'Well, that's more than I have in him.' I made light of the encounter. She did take the precaution of winding his lead shorter, and jerking him towards her, instead of allowing him to discover more about me.

But the Alsatian's strength and determination were greater than hers. Round the corner breezily strode the Insurance Man. With his dark good looks he was a welcome visitor where e'er he walked, or so he thought.

How false an assumption! The dog turned his attention from me, and with a vicious lunge attacked the Insurance Man. Another inch more lead and we'd have seen the chap minus his trousers. Or something.

John the gardener came strolling past, hands in corduroy pockets as usual. He winked broadly at me.

'Damned good guard dogs those, Lollipop!' I nearly cried. Never for him to call me 'Lollipop' again…

Only one more crossing to go. Nobody knew. They probably thought I was a fixture for another year.

When I arrived home there was a slim white envelope on the doormat. I tore it open eagerly. It was from the BBC in Manchester.

'12th January 1967

Dear Mrs Wheeler,

This is just to let you know that we would like to use your talk "Married Ladies Concerts – Thirties Style" in our "Home this Afternoon" programme on January 27th and we are asking one of our professional readers to record it for us.

You will be hearing shortly about the fee from our Copyright Department, and I do hope you will enjoy listening to the programme.

Yours sincerely,

Denness Roylance
(Assistant "Home this Afternoon")
North Region'

When I did hear, the fee was 10 guineas – more that three times what I earned on the crossing for a week's work.

Yet what a turmoil of emotions surged within me as the final moments ticked away. I was upset that I wouldn't be seeing the familiar faces – gardener John, Brown Grandad and Beverley, to name but a few – with whom I chatted daily. Each day had been like coming to the end of a story, but knowing that tomorrow I'd find out what happened next. And when you are not in regular contact with people, the link weakens and eventually breaks. It's a bit like listening to conversations on a bus – just when the most interesting part is about to be disclosed, one has to get off the bus, the destination having been reached.

The time had come for me to get off, not the bus, but the crossing. What if I'd given up a regular income – such as it was – for the precarious nature of freelance writing? What if we couldn't pay off the moneylenders eventually? What if…? Yet I was eternally grateful that, having taken the risk of become a Lollipop Lady almost a year ago, I had had the experience and made the contacts that proved there are far worse problems than getting into a financial fix. With hard work, perseverance, humour, and a bit of luck, it could be overcome, even though it might take years. Moneylenders can drain the life blood out of a victim – financially and emotionally. But health problems, disabilities, blindness, cancer, and all the other worries I had come across as a Lollipop Lady, listening to the troubles of others, can sometimes never be overcome, unless a miracle happens.

I had health, my husband and children, Prince the cat – and Roddy from the bungalow opposite – as supports along the pathway of life. I was not alone, as poor old Mrs Jackson, Mrs Wibley and the other widows were. Love and companionship is worth far more than riches.

I had learned more tolerance from rubbing shoulders with the ordinary man, woman and child on the street than ever I had before I was a Lollipop Lady. Certainly I'd never look down on anyone working as one. Really, after experiencing that life, I think they *all* deserve a mention in the Honours List! Yet I hoped that the letter from the BBC was a sign that the right decision had been taken.

It's always sad saying goodbye. Yet I was relieved to be leaving with an unblemished record. No accidents had been caused through any fault of mine. And, thank God, I had never missed being at the crossing on time.

The last mother and child I escorted over 'my' crossing were unaware that it was the last time for me. The mother smiled and thanked me warmly as we reached the opposite side of the road.

'I must tell you, Mrs Wheeler, my little girl thinks you're a lovely Lollipop Lady!'

No tribute could have made me happier as I carried the 'STOP – CHILDREN' crossing pole – dear Lollipop – down the snicket for the very last time, to be picked up by a new Lollipop Man next morning.

With tears in my eyes I propped her against the wall, gazed at her, then kissed her lightly on her dirty face.

'Good luck, Lollipop – you'll be all right,' I whispered.

After all, she had been my companion in all kinds of weather. But now, the cavalcade was over.

Other books from
The **NOSTALGIA** *Collection*

OI JIMMY KNACKER
A memoir of an
East Ender's childhood
Ken Kimberley

More than 40 incidents that remain strong in Ken's memory are illustrated by astonishingly detailed watercolours that draw the reader immediately into that magical childhood world. Accompanying each picture is an evocative pen portrait recounting the story behind it. The result is a book that truly captures the character, life and colour of the old East End.

1 85794 120 9   **Hardback**   **£16.99**

HEAVO, HEAVO, LASH UP AND STOW!
Memoirs of an East Ender's war
Ken Kimberley

In *Oi Jimmy Knacker* Ken Kimberley recounted his memories of a childhood in the pre-war East End of London. *Heavo, Heavo, Lash up and Stow* continues his story, relating his experiences in the Royal Navy during the Second World War.

Again, the book is illustrated in full colour throughout by Ken's own beautiful paintings and pen-and-ink sketches.

1 85794 134 9   **Hardback**   **£16.99**

KNOCK DOWN GINGER
Illustrated tales from younger days
Ken Kimberley

Oi Jimmy Knacker was so successful that his and his readers' further memories have provided this 'postscript', containing many new paintings as well as poignant and humorous recollections of a London and a way of life long gone.

1 85794 222 1   **Paperback**   **£14.99**

Other books from
The NOSTALGIA *Collection*

THE BIRDWATCHER
and other tales from the footplate
Stan Wilson

Percy Sidebottom, the birdwatcher – and we're not referring to our feathered friends here – is just one of the more outrageously bizarre members of the steam age railway fraternity encountered in this funny, nostalgic and irreverent anthology. Although all the characters are fictitious, former railwayman Stan Wilson has drawn them all faithfully from life.

1 85794 153 5   Paperback   £15.99

TICKET TO THE GALLOWS
and other villainous tales from the tracks
Barry Herbert

This entertaining, intriguing and sometimes chilling catalogue of more than 40 real-life crime tales with a railway setting introduces us to a rich and varied rogues' gallery of thieves, vandals, arsonists and murderers, from the birth of Britain's railways to the present day.

1 85794 088 1   Paperback   £14.99

HOME SWEET HOME
A nostalgic look at domestic duties since 1945
Maggie Brogan

A fascinating and highly illustrated survey of everyday home life over the last 50 years. Both humorous and packed with insights, it shows just how much our lives have been shaped by the post-war domestic revolution in cooking, cleaning, washing, and much more. Illustrated throughout by a remarkable collection of photographs and period advertisements.

1 85895 118 6   Paperback   £15.99